SO YOU THINK YOU'RE A
PHILADELPHIA
FLYERS
FAN?

SO YOU THINK YOU'RE A
PHILADELPHIA
FLYERS
FAN?

**STARS, STATS, RECORDS,
AND MEMORIES
FOR TRUE DIEHARDS**

SKIP CLAYTON
FOREWORD BY BILL CLEMENT

Sports Publishing books may be purchased in bulk at special discounts for sales promotion, corporate gifts, fund-raising, or educational purposes. Special editions can also be created to specifications. For details, contact the Special Sales Department, Sports Publishing, 307 West 36th Street, 11th Floor, New York, NY 10018 or sportspubbooks@skyhorsepublishing.com.

Sports Publishing® is a registered trademark of Skyhorse Publishing, Inc.®, a Delaware corporation.

Visit our website at www.sportspubbooks.com.

10 9 8 7 6 5 4 3 2 1

Library of Congress Cataloging-in-Publication Data is available on file.

Series design by Tom Lau
Cover photo: AP Images

Print ISBN: 978-1-68358-242-7
Ebook ISBN: 978-1-68358-243-4

Printed in the United States of America

To my wife, Joanne, who is a tower of strength and is always there for me when needed, especially for all the hours that it took to write this book. She has always been behind me 100 percent during all our time together and is a great wife and mother.

In the memory of my parents, Natalie and Bill, who I still miss and they both always taught me the difference between right and wrong. My dad not only took me to Phillies and Eagles games, we also went to see the Ramblers and Flyers. They always came out to see me play baseball and basketball and were always there for me.

Also, in memory of my grandmothers, Louise Goelitz, Edna Clayton, and my grandfather George P. Clayton, who went to Phillies games with me and my dad and came to see me play baseball. I remember all the great times at their homes.

I love them all.

Acknowledgments

I would like to thank Zack Hill and Brian Smith of the Flyers for their research help and Ben Reese for his assistance.

Among the publications that were of great assistance were the *2017–18 Philadelphia Flyers Media Guide*, *Full Spectrum* by Jay Greenberg, *Flyer Lives* by Jakki Clarke, and the *National Hockey League Official Guide & Record Book 2018*.

Contents

Foreword

By Bill Clement

How many walking, talking "sports encyclopedias" do you know? If you've ever spent time around Skip Clayton, you can say you have met at least one.

I have always maintained that our ability to retain knowledge is directly proportionate to our interest level. Well, for as long as I can remember, Skip's appetite for Philadelphia sports has been insatiable. When our Broad Street Bullies teams began marching (okay, skating) towards Stanley Cups, the horde of media types that followed us steadily grew. New faces . . . new names. "Who is that guy?" we would ask one another and often, nobody had an answer.

That wasn't the case when we saw Skip. He was (and still is) a fixture on the sports scene and he usually wore his passion for Philly sports on his sleeve. Never short of opinions, ideas, obtuse notions, and obscure factoids, Skip Clayton was and always has been a thread that runs through the fabric of Philadelphia's sports culture.

Time doesn't stand still, and our world of sports looks nothing like it did back in the day.

In many respects, we were all in it together—players, media, fans . . . all of us. It was *our* city against the other cities. What endeared Skip to our Flyers teams was that we could trust him. We were never concerned that he would take sensitive information or observations and try to spin them into something he could use for personal gain. We always knew Skip was one of us.

Taking a stroll back through Flyers memory lane with Skip Clayton is awesome because he spans as many decades following the Flyers as anybody alive. I continue to marvel at his ability to recall specifics that bring facts, numbers, and people to life. I'm also grateful for being given another chance to relive a time, a place, or an incident that otherwise might continue to exist only as a vague memory in the corner of my mind.

Young or old, there is something in these pages for all of us. Thank you, Skip!

—Bill Clement
Two-time Stanley Cup Winner
Color Analyst, NBC Sports Philadelphia

Introduction

For many years, the National Hockey League only had six teams. The nearest city Philadelphia fans could see an NHL game was in New York. Only once did Philadelphia have a team in the NHL, the Philadelphia Quakers in 1930–31. They lasted one year and only won four of 44 games. Philadelphia had numerous minor league teams, however.

It began with the Arrows who began play in 1927 in the Canadian-American Hockey League and ended with the Ramblers who set up shop in the 1955–56 season and stayed for nine years before moving across the river to New Jersey.

The first team I remember was the Rockets in the American Hockey League, who played in the City of Brotherly Love from 1946–47 until 1948–49. I never saw them play and it wasn't until 1956 that I saw my first hockey game. The Philadelphia Ramblers joined the Eastern Hockey League in the 1955–56 season. I saw them beat the Johnstown Jets, 8–6. The game was tied, 5–5, after two periods when the Ramblers scored three straight goals. Jimmy Moore scored twice and Rollie Savard notched the other between Moore's pair. There were 2,701 fans at my first game. If you brought your skates, you could to go out on the ice and skate after the game. I enjoyed watching the Ramblers with players such as Ray Crew, Art Dorrington, Rocky Rukavina, and Ivan Walmsley. The first year, the Ramblers didn't make the playoffs, but the second year they reached the finals, losing to the Charlotte Clippers.

One problem that the Ramblers and all the teams before them was having to play at the Philadelphia Arena at 45th and Market Streets. The basketball Warriors and 76ers also played there at times. It was a small building seating about 5,500 for hockey and 6,600 for basketball and wasn't in the best of shape. At the same time, there wasn't a bad seat in the building.

When the NHL expanded for the 1967–68 season, they added six teams, not one or two at a time. When the NFL started expanding in 1960, they only had 12 teams and would add one or two teams at a time while Major League Baseball added two teams in each league, bringing their total to ten in each league by 1962. The NHL doubled in size and there were cities that wanted a team in the worst way. Philadelphia was not considered a top choice to add an expansion team. Their minor-league teams hadn't drawn well and one of the things that the Flyers needed to get into the National Hockey League was a new building. The Spectrum was erected and had over 14,000 seats.

Putting teams in Los Angeles and Oakland was a great start, giving the league exposure on the West Coast. Two teams were added in St. Louis and Minnesota. There were also two teams added in the East, Pittsburgh and Philadelphia, who beat out Baltimore for the final spot.

Ed Snider was at the Boston Garden for a basketball game between the 76ers and Celtics one afternoon and while leaving the arena, saw a long line of fans lining up for that evening's Bruins game. The Bruins failed to make the playoffs for eight consecutive seasons beginning in 1959–60, but they frequently sold out their games. During that same time span, the Celtics won seven National Basketball Association championships but were not filling the Garden on a regular basis.

Snider decided that Philadelphia should have an NHL team and was able to secure a franchise after Jerry Wolman built the Spectrum. The six new teams were all placed in the same division and the Flyers went out and finished in first place. Many thought the Flyers would stay for one year and move to another city. That was hardly the case. During the first season, the Flyers won back-to-back games over Chicago and Toronto before sellout crowds in February, ending any thoughts they would be in Philadelphia for one year. Attendance increased each year.

The following season, when I became the Sports Director of WRCP Radio in Philadelphia and started covering sports for the ABC Radio Network, I received my first press credential from any of the four professional teams in Philadelphia and the first and it was from the Flyers. I still have that first credential. Finally, I would see my first NHL game from the press box after watching from the stands the year before. I was there Opening Night in October 1968 and with Bernie Parent in net, the Flyers shut out Pittsburgh, 3–0. It wasn't until their sixth season that they had a winning season and won a playoff series. The next three years were the greatest in Flyers history. First, they won their first Stanley Cup in just their seventh season and won it again the following year. Although they lost the finals in 1976 to Montreal (who started a run of four straight Stanley Cups), the prestige of the league was at stake during that season when the Soviet Red Army Team came over and played four games. They had beaten the Boston Bruins, New York Rangers, and tied the Montreal Canadiens. At the same time, a second team from Russia, the Wings, came over and won three of its four games.

Although the Flyers were unpopular throughout the National Hockey League, the whole league became fans of the team for one day. Everyone realized the NHL needed the Flyers to win this game which they did with ease, 4–1.

Seeing them win the Stanley Cup in 1974 was my biggest thrill covering the Flyers and the win close to two years later over the Soviets was my second biggest.

Over the years that I covered the team, I have seen some highs and lows but mostly highs. Despite winning only two Stanley Cups, they made it back to the finals six times afterwards. The Flyers have been a great team to cover throughout their history.

FIRST PERIOD

We begin with easier questions. They cover the time the Flyers were born in 1967 and goes through the 51 seasons the Flyers have been in the NHL.

(Answers begin on page 5)

1 What was the nickname of the Philadelphia NHL team in 1930–31?

2 Who were the other teams that joined the Flyers in 1967–68 when the NHL added six teams?

3 Who was the first player that the Flyers chose in the expansion draft and from what team?

4 Which team did the Flyers pick the most players from in the expansion draft?

5 Match these Flyers with the year they were drafted

Bill Barber	1969
Simon Gagne	2006
Claude Giroux	1998
Paul Holmgren	1982
Ken Linseman	1975
Dave Schultz	1972
Ron Sutter	1978

6 Match these Flyers with the round they were drafted

Jeff Carter, 2003	Round 3
Bill Clement, 1970	Round 8
Chris Therien, 1990	Round 2
Rick Tocchet, 1983	Round 6
Pelle Eklund, 1983	Round 1

7 Match the Flyers goalie with the round he was drafted

Brian Boucher	Round 8
Ron Hextall	Round 4
Pelle Lindbergh	Round 6
Pete Peeters	Round 1
Dominic Roussel	Round 11
Rick St. Croix	Round 2
Tommy Soderstrom	Round 3

8 In what round was Bobby Clarke drafted?

9 What teams did the Flyers trade with to acquire the following players?

Rod Brind'Amour	Pittsburgh
Bob Dailey	Montreal
Mark Howe	St. Louis
Reggie Leach	Vancouver
John LeClair	Hartford
Mark Recchi	California

10 What team did the Flyers play in their first National Hockey League game?

11 Who did the Flyers beat for their first National Hockey League win?

12 Who was the Flyers' first opponent at the Spectrum?

13 Which goalie recorded the first Flyers shutout?

14 Who was the first Original Six team to play against the Flyers?

15 Who was the first Original Six team to lose to the Flyers?

16 Who was the first Flyers captain?

17 What Original Six team did the Flyers beat three out of four times in their first season?

18 When Keith Allen conducted his first NHL amateur draft in 1970, who was the first player he picked?

19 Against which team did Bernie Parent record his first shutout with the Flyers?

20 The Flyers have had 18 coaches. Only seven won their first game behind the bench. Who were they?

21 Five Flyers coaches had also played for the team. Who were they?

22 One Flyers owner and two general managers made the Hockey Hall of Fame as builders. Who were they?

23 Four Flyers coaches made the Hall of Fame as builders. Name them.

24 Who is the only Flyers coach to win a Stanley Cup with another team after leaving Philadelphia?

25 Four coaches won the Calder Cup championship in the American Hockey League coaching a Flyers farm team. Who were they?

FIRST PERIOD ANSWERS

1 Quakers.

Pittsburgh moved its NHL franchise to Philadelphia in 1931, but the season was far from a success. The Quakers tied the record set by the 1919–20 Quebec Bulldogs for the fewest wins for a team playing a full season with four. They set the record for the lowest winning percentage with .136 (4–36–4) which was broken 44 years later by the Washington Capitals with .131. Ironically, Pittsburgh which carried the same nickname as the baseball team, the Pirates, were only 5–36–3 in its final season in the Iron City.

The first minor league team in Philadelphia was the Arrows who played eight seasons in the Canadian-American Hockey League beginning in 1927. They changed their name to the Ramblers in 1935 and played four seasons in the Canadian-American Hockey League before joining the American Hockey League for two seasons. The Rockets began play in the AHL in 1946–47. After three years, only 42 wins and no playoff appearances, the team folded. The next minor league entry was another Ramblers team which played in Philadelphia nine seasons in the Eastern Hockey League. None of those teams drew well playing in the Philadelphia Arena. Philadelphia had a reputation of not being a good hockey town but that changed when the Flyers joined the NHL.

2 Los Angeles, Minnesota, Oakland, Pittsburgh, and St. Louis.

Numerous cities were seeking a National Hockey League team. The NHL decided to go coast to coast when it expanded in 1967. It added two teams on the West Coast, the Los Angeles Kings and the California Seals. Two teams were added in the Midwest, the St. Louis Blues and the Minnesota North Stars. The two Eastern teams were the Flyers and the Pittsburgh Penguins. This meant that Philadelphia, Los Angeles, Oakland (Bay Area), Pittsburgh, and St. Louis all became four-major team sports markets as Pittsburgh and Minnesota also had teams in the new American Basketball Association. The NHL also increased its schedule from 70 to 74 games. It was decided to put all the new teams in the West Division and the original six teams would make up the East Division. The new teams would play each other 10 times and the established clubs four times.

3 Bernie Parent from Boston.

When the expansion draft began, the first two rounds were to select goalies. The Flyers drafted after Los Angeles who took future Hall of Famer Terry Sawchuk. Another future Hall of Fame goaltender, Glenn Hall, was available, but the Flyers tabbed Parent. In the second round, the Flyers still drafting for the future, went back to Boston and took Doug Favell. Both had celebrated their twenty-second birthdays two days apart in April. When the numbers were assigned to the players, Favell got number one which most goalies in the NHL were wearing at the time and Parent was given number 30.

Parent had seen action the two previous seasons with the Bruins and their farm team in Oklahoma City while Favell was also at Oklahoma and didn't make his NHL debut until he played for the Flyers. Each goaltender posted four shutouts. Favell had a goals-against average of 2.27 which turned out to be his best. Meanwhile, Parent who had an average of 2.49 would go onto to have a Hall of Fame career in two stints with the Flyers and one with Toronto playing with his idol, Jacques Plante, who played a big part in helping him.

Interestingly, when the Philadelphia Wings made their debut in the National Lacrosse League in 1974, they played their first game at the Spectrum hours after the Flyers won their first Stanley Cup and Favell was one of the Wings' players.

4 The Boston Bruins with seven of their 20 picks.

After the Flyers took Parent and Favell from Boston, they later selected Joe Watson in the fourth round, Dick Cherry in round 11, Gary Dornhoefer in the 14th round, and Forbes Kennedy in the 15th round. The last player the Flyers picked from Boston was Keith Wright in the 19th round.

The Flyers took four players from Chicago beginning with Ed Van Impe in the third round, followed by Lou Angotti, in round six, John Miszuk in round nine, and Pat Hannigan in the 16th round. The Flyers also took four players from Montreal beginning with Leon Rochefort in round seven and Garry Peters three rounds later. Jean Gauthier was taken in the 12th round and Bob Courcy in the 18th round. The Maple Leafs, who won the last Stanley Cup before expansion, lost two players to the Flyers, Brit Selby in round five and Don Blackburn in round eight. The New York Rangers also lost two players to the Flyers as Jimmy Johnson was taken in the 13th round and Terry Ball was taken in the 20th and final round. The Flyers only drafted one player from Detroit, Dwight Carruthers in the 17th round.

5 Dave Schultz   1969
   Bill Barber   1972
   Paul Holmgren   1975
   Ken Linesman   1978
   Ron Sutter   1982
   Simon Gagne   1998
   Claude Giroux   2006

The 1969 draft had produced Bobby Clarke, but the Flyers also picked Dave Schultz in the fifth round and Don Saleski in the sixth. Schultz made sure that the Flyers weren't going to be pushed around anymore when he joined the team. One weakness of the Flyers in their two seasons was they weren't big enough or strong enough, especially against St. Louis who dominated them. Ed Snider told his general manager and scouting department to get some tough guys in. The fifth player they took in the 1969 draft was Schultz. Nobody knew it at time, but the Broad Street Bullies were starting to be assembled. Schultz played one game in 1972 and was with the team for the next four years, leading the league in penalty minutes in three of them. His high was 472 minutes in 1975, still an NHL record. When the Flyers defeated the Atlanta Flames in four straight in the first round of the 1974 Stanley Cup playoffs, they had to win the fourth game in overtime, 4–3, and it was Schultz who scored the game-winner with assists to Bobby Clarke and Bill Flett. When the Flyers won Game Two of the Stanley Cup Finals in Boston, it was the same three players on the winning goal in overtime, only it was Clarke that scored the game-winner and Schultz and Flett assisted. Schultz was traded to the Los Angeles Kings after the 1975-76 season. He was inducted into the Flyers Hall of Fame in 2009.

Bill Barber was drafted in 1972 and began his professional career with the Richmond Robins, the Flyers' top minor league team. Then came the call to join the Flyers and Barber never looked back. His career was cut short by knee injuries but, while he was with the team, he set the club record for the most goals with 420 and is second in points with 883. Barber is also second in games played with 903. One of his most famous goals came with Team Canada in the 1976 Canada Cup. Team Canada was trailing by a goal against Czechoslovakia in the final game when Barber scored to tie the game and send it into overtime where Team Canada went onto win.

Barber had reconstructive knee surgery in the spring of 1984, but never played again, retiring at the age of thirty-two. His days as a player were over, but he began his coaching career with a short stint with the Flyers' top farm team in Hershey in 1984–85 before joining the Flyers' coaching staff the following year. He became an assistant coach with the Flyers, then coached the Phantoms to the 1998 Calder Cup championship in the American Hockey League and later coached the Flyers for close to two years. He was inducted into the Flyers Hall of Fame in 1989, joining Ed Snider and Keith Allen in the second class. A year later, Barber was inducted into the Hockey Hall of Fame and his number seven was retired by the Flyers.

Paul Holmgren was drafted in 1975 and played one game with the Flyers in 1975–76. He came up for good the following year and remained with the team until he was traded to the Minnesota North Stars during the 1983–84 season. When he left Philadelphia, he was club's all-time leader in penalty minutes with 1,600. Holmgren played 500 games and was a big part of the team's unbeaten streak of 35 straight games during the 1979–80 season. When he retired as player after the

1984–85 season, he rejoined the Flyers as an assistant coach for three years before succeeding Mike Keenan as head coach. Holmgren was let go as coach after 24 games in his fourth season behind the bench. He wasn't out of work long, later becoming the coach and general manager of Hartford. When the Whalers sent Holmgren packing, he quickly rejoined the Flyers in their front office. After holding down different positions, he was elevated to general manager, replacing Bobby Clarke who stepped down during the 2006–07 season. On May 7, 2014, Holmgren became president of the Flyers and takes care of the business and hockey operations of the team.

Ken Linseman was drafted by the Flyers in the first round in 1978. The Flyers had two first-round picks that year and took Behn Wilson one spot ahead of Linseman. Nicknamed "The Rat" for the way he could agitate the opposing team to take penalties, Linseman started the 1978–79 season with the Flyers' top farm team, the Maine Mariners, but after 38 games, he was called up to the Flyers. He stayed with the team through the 1981–82 season when he was traded to the Hartford Whalers in a deal that brought future Hall of Famer Mark Howe to Philadelphia. This had to rank as Keith Allen's second-best trade only behind the trade that bought Bernie Parent back to Philadelphia. Linseman tied Clarke for the most assists in 1979–80 with 57 and he led the club in assists and points two years later in his final season with Philadelphia.

Ron Sutter's name was called out in the 1982 draft with the fourth overall pick. The 10th player taken in the first round of the draft was Ron's twin brother, Rich by Pittsburgh. Ron and Rich were two of six brothers that played in the National Hockey League; the others were Brian, Brent, Darryl, and Duane. Ron was drafted highest of the six. A seventh brother, Gary, who was the oldest, turned down the chance to play. Rich was traded to the Flyers during the 1983–84 season and the two brothers played three years together before Rich was sent to Vancouver. Ron and Rich never turned to coaching but the other four brothers did. Darryl had the most success, winning the Stanley Cup with Los Angeles in 2012 and 2014. A second generation of Sutters made it to the National Hockey League as three of Ron's nephews; Brandon, Brett, and Brody, have seen ice time.

Simon Gagne was drafted by the Flyers in 1998 and joined the club for the 1999–2000 season, being named to the NHL All-Rookie Team. After one year at center, Gagne was switched to left wing and played on a line with Mark Recchi and Keith Primeau. After the lockout season of 2004–05, Gagne teamed up with Peter Forsberg and Mike Knuble on the Deuces Wild Line. Gagne wore number 12, Forsberg 21 and Knuble 22. Gagne played 11 seasons with the Flyers and scored 264 goals, had 271 assists and 535 points. He saw action in 691 games. In Gagne's final season with the Flyers (2009–10), he started the big comeback against the Bruins in the playoffs after the Flyers had lost the first three games. Gagne scored the game-winning goal in overtime in Game Four and had two goals in the fifth game. When the Flyers won the seventh game in Boston and became the third NHL team to come back from a 3–0 series deficit, Gagne scored the game winning-goal with 7:08 left in the third period. After the season, he was traded to Tampa Bay and played on the Los Angeles Kings' first Stanley Cup champion two years later. He was traded back to the Flyers from Los Angeles during the 2012–13 season.

Claude Giroux was selected 22nd overall in the first round of the 2006 draft. Giroux made it up to the Flyers in 2007–08 and the following year divided his time between the Flyers and the Phantoms. When he was recalled that year, he was back with the Flyers for good. During his career with the Flyers, Giroux became the fourth player in club history to have two straight seasons with 50 or more assists joining Bobby Clarke, Brian Propp, and Mark Recchi. He had 65 assists in 2011–12, becoming the seventh player in Flyers history to record 60 or more assists in a season. Giroux also led the league in power play points with 38, assisting on 32 goals while scoring six times. Giroux was named the 19th captain in Flyers history during the 2012–13 season.

6 Jeff Carter   Round 1
   Bill Clement   Round 2
   Chris Therien   Round 3
   Rick Tocchet   Round 6
   Pelle Eklund   Round 8

Sometimes your top players aren't your first- or second-round draft picks. There have been other times when a number-one choice didn't make the club. Jeff Carter was one of those number-one picks that made it big when he was selected in the first round of the 2003 draft. After leading the Philadelphia

Phantoms to the Calder Cup championship in 2005, Carter spent six seasons with the Flyers before being traded to Columbus after the 2010–11 season. Two years earlier, Carter had his best season with the Flyers when he recorded 84 points. He was second in the NHL in goals scored with 46 and led in game-winning goals with 12. Late in his only season (2011–12) with the Blue Jackets, he was traded to Los Angeles and helped the Kings win the Stanley Cup in 2012 and 2014.

The Flyers didn't have a first-round draft choice in 1970, but had to wait until the second round. When the Flyers' turn came to make a selection, they chose Bill Clement who made it up to the Flyers during the 1971–72 season and stayed through the 1974–75 season. He helped the Flyers win their Stanley Cup championships in 1974 and 1975. In the sixth and deciding game in the 1975 finals at Buffalo, Clement scored an insurance goal with 2:47 left as the Flyers won the game, 2–0, and won the clinching game on a Bernie Parent shutout for the second straight year. Shortly after the season ended, Clement was traded to Washington. After less than one season with the Capitals, he spent seven seasons with the Atlanta/Calgary Flames. Afterwards, Clement turned to broadcasting and has worked for ESPN, ABC, NBC, Versus, TNT, and is currently working for NBC Sports Philadelphia and hosts an ice hockey program every Wednesday night on WBCB Radio in Levittown.

Chris Therien was drafted in the third round in 1990 draft and spent close to 11 seasons with the Flyers. He made the All-NHL Rookie team in 1994-95. Due to the lockout and a shortened 48-game season, Therien started the season with the Flyers' top farm team, the Hershey Bears. Towards the end of the 2003–04 season, he was traded to Dallas and finished the season there, playing 11 games. The 2004–05 NHL season was cancelled and when play resumed the following season, he returned to the Flyers but played only 47 games, calling it a season and later a career after suffering a head injury. Therien holds the club record for most games played by a defenseman with 753, breaking the previous record of 746 set by Joe Watson. Nicknamed Bundy after the character Al Bundy from the television program *Married . . . With Children*, Therien is the color analyst on the Flyers' broadcast team with play-by-play announcer, Jim Jackson.

Rick Tocchet was taken by the Flyers in the sixth round in 1983. Tocchet joined the Flyers in 1984–85 and spent his first eight NHL seasons in Philadelphia, helping the team reach the Stanley Cup Finals in 1985 and 1987. During the 1991–92 season, he was traded to Pittsburgh and helped the Penguins win the Stanley Cup. After leaving Pittsburgh, Tocchet played with Los Angeles, Boston, Washington, and Phoenix before finishing his career back in Philadelphia when he was traded by the Coyotes during the 1999–2000 season. Tocchet called it a career 14 games into the 2001–02 season, He set the Flyers record for the most penalty minutes in a career with 1,815.

Pelle Eklund wasn't drafted by the Flyers until the eighth round in 1983 but went on to have an outstanding nine-year career in Philadelphia before he was dealt to the Dallas Stars late in the 1993–94 season which turned out to be his last in the NHL. Eklund broke in with the Flyers in 1985–86, picking up 15 goals and 51 assists, the most by any rookie that season and he was third in rookie points behind Kjell Dahlin of Montreal and Gary Suter of Calgary. He was one of least penalized players in the NHL and collected 50 assists in a season three times.

7 Brian Boucher   Round 1
Pelle Lindbergh   Round 2
Dominic Roussel   Round 3
Rick St. Croix   Round 4
Ron Hextall   Round 6
Pete Peeters   Round 8
Tommy Soderstrom   Round 11

In 1995, Brian Boucher became the first of only two goalies that the Flyers have ever selected in the first round of the NHL draft. (The other was Maxime Quellet four years later.) He joined the team in 1999–2000 and made the NHL All-Rookie team. Boucher helped the Flyers advance to the Eastern Conference finals before they lost to the New Jersey Devils in seven games, allowing an average of only 2.03 goals per game in the playoffs. He spent 13 seasons in the NHL, including three tours of duty with the Flyers, also backstopping Phoenix, Calgary, Chicago, and San Jose. Boucher came back to the Flyers for two years starting in 2009–10 before spending one year with Carolina. Boucher returned to play four games in 2012–13 before hanging up the skates for good. In 174 games with Philadelphia, Boucher gave up an average of 2.50 goals per game.

Pelle Lindbergh was selected in the second round of the 1979 draft and joined the Flyers for eight games in 1981–82. The following year, Lindbergh made the NHL All-Rookie Team and was selected to play in the All-Star Game. Two years later, Lindbergh won 40 games and the Vezina Trophy. The Flyers finished in first place and led the league with the most points. In the playoffs, the Flyers eliminated the Islanders, who had been to the finals the previous five years, in five games. Lindbergh registered shutouts in Game One, 3–0, and in the fifth game,

1–0. After beating Quebec to move onto the finals, Edmonton took out the Flyers in five games to win its second straight Stanley Cup.

The Flyers went into the next season with high hopes of winning the Stanley Cup for the first time in 11 years, but bad news came after only 14 games of the regular season. The Flyers had beaten Boston, 5–3, on a Saturday night at the Spectrum. Lindbergh didn't play in that game. In the early hours of the following morning, Lindbergh was driving his Porsche 930 Turbo and struck a wall and was critically injured. Two other passengers in the car were injured. Two hours later, Lindbergh was declared brain dead. After his parents arrived from Sweden, he was taken off life support and died. He was still voted to the Wales Conference All Star team. The Pelle Lindbergh Memorial Trophy has been awarded annually since 1993–94 to the most improved Flyers player as voted by his teammates.

Dominic Roussel was drafted in the third round in 1988 and joined the Flyers in 1991–92 as a backup to Ron Hextall. After the season, Hextall was traded along with five other players, the Flyers' first-round draft picks in 1993 and 1994, and $15 million to Quebec for Eric Lindros. Roussel split playing time with Tommy Soderstrom and Stephane Beauregard the following season and was the No. 1 goaltender in 1993–94. After seeing limited action the next two seasons, Roussel was traded to Winnipeg for goaltender Tim Cheveldae and a third-round draft choice in 1996. At the end of the year, he re-signed with the Flyers but played with the Phantoms. Roussel finished his NHL career playing for Anaheim and Edmonton.

Rick St. Croix was selected in the fourth round of the 1975 draft and made his Philadelphia debut during the 1977–78 season, playing seven games. He played two more games the

following season and one game in 1979–80. He spent most of those first three years with the Maine Mariners and the Philadelphia Firebirds in the AHL. St. Croix's first full season with the Flyers was in 1980–81 when he divided his playing time with Pete Peeters and Phil Myre. During the 1982–83 season, he was traded to Toronto for goaltender Michel Larocque.

Ron Hextall was drafted in the sixth round in 1982. After Pelle Lindbergh's tragic death in 1985, Bob Froese, who was the starter in the majority of the games two years earlier, took over as goalie while Darren Jensen was called up from the minors. After playing three games at the start of the 1986–87 season, Froese was traded to the New York Rangers for Kjell Samuelsson and a 1989 second-round draft choice. Hextall took over as the starter right away with Glenn Resch as the backup and won the Vezina Trophy, Conn Smythe Trophy, was named a first team NHL All-Star and made the NHL All-Rookie team.

Hextall had two tours of duty with the Flyers. He was traded to Quebec in 1992 in a blockbuster trade that also sent Mike Ricci, Peter Forsberg, Steve Duchesne, Kerry Huffman, Chris Simon, the Flyers' first-round draft picks in 1993 and 1994, and $15 million for Eric Lindros. After spending two seasons with Quebec and the New York Islanders, Hextall returned to the Flyers and played five more seasons, setting the club records for goaltenders for most wins with 240 and most games played with 489. He became the Flyers' seventh general manager on May 7, 2014, and was the third former Flyers player to assume this post.

Pete Peeters was taken in the eighth round of the 1977 draft and he wasn't even the first goalie the Flyers drafted that year. In the fourth round, they selected Yves Guillemette who never played in the National Hockey League. Peeters came up during the 1978–79 season after a career-ending injury sidelined Bernie Parent. Peeters went on to post 29 of the club's 48 wins the following year when the Flyers, after splitting their first two games, went on a 35-game unbeaten streak. He played in the All-Star game that year and the following season as well. After the 1981–82 season, Peeters was traded to Boston for Brad McCrimmon. He rejoined the Flyers in 1989–90 as a free agent but after two seasons, he retired. Peeters ranks fifth in Flyers history for most games played by a goalie with 179.

Tommy Soderstrom only spent two seasons with the Flyers, beginning in the 1992–93 season. Drafted in the 11th round in 1990, he was traded to the New York Islanders in 1994, in a deal for Hextall and a sixth-round draft pick. Soderstrom had five shutouts in his rookie season, second best in the league, and two behind the leader, Ed Belfour of Chicago. After two years with the Islanders, Soderstrom was out of the league.

8 Second round.

The Flyers selected Bob Currier with their first draft pick (sixth overall) in 1969. By the time the second round began, Clarke was still available. In the first round, Boston passed on Clarke three times, and Montreal and the Rangers twice. When the second round began, Minnesota, Pittsburgh and Los Angeles passed on Clarke. Teams were afraid of taking Clarke with a high draft pick because he was diabetic. When the Flyers took Clarke, Detroit came over and offered the Flyers two players right off the bat. They say that sometimes the best trades are the ones you don't make, and the Flyers turned down that deal in a hurry.

9 Reggie Leach, California Seals, May 24, 1974
Bob Dailey, Vancouver January 20, 1977
Mark Howe, Hartford, August 19, 1982
Rod Brind'Amour, St. Louis, September 22, 1991
Mark Recchi, Pittsburgh, February 19, 1992
John LeClair, Montreal, February 9, 1995

The parade was hardly over after the Flyers won their first Stanley Cup and general manager, Keith Allen had already begun thinking about winning another. Right wing Reggie Leach was the player that Allen was trying to get from California. Leach was a former junior linemate of Bobby Clarke at Flin Flon. He was drafted by Boston in 1970, played parts of two seasons with Bruins, and was traded to the Seals with 17 games to go in the 1971–72 season. In his three years on the West Coast, Leach scored 51 goals in 171 games. The Seals won only 29 games in Leach's last two years. Allen sent Larry Wright, Al MacAdam, and a first round draft choice (Ron Chipperfield) to the Seals. In his first year with the Flyers, Leach scored 45 goals and helped the team win the Stanley Cup for the second straight season. He spent eight years with the Flyers and set the record for the most goals scored in a season with 61 in 1975–76. He is seventh in club history in goals scored with 306. Leach was inducted into the Flyers Hall of Fame in 1992.

Sometimes you wonder when you trade two players for one if you got the better deal. Keith Allen did that when he traded two defensemen, Larry Goodenough and Jack McIlhargey to Vancouver for Bob Dailey, another defenseman, on January 20, 1977. Once again, Keith Allen kept adding to his nickname, Keith the Thief. Dailey set club records at the time for most goals by a defenseman with 21 and most points with 57 in 1977–78. He was injured during the 1980–81 season and played only 53 games. In the 12th game of the following season, Dailey shattered his ankle in three places when he caught a rut in the ice in a game at Buffalo. It took three screws to repair his ankle and ended his career at only twenty-eight. He spent six years with the Flyers, but only three full seasons and parts of three others. Dailey played only 304 games with Philadelphia, scored 56 goals and had 138 assists and played in two All-Star Games.

With the loss of a career-ending injury to Dailey, Allen was in the market for a defenseman and he pulled off another great trade, getting Mark Howe, son of Hall of Famer Gordie Howe, from the Whalers in 1982. To get Howe and a third-round draft pick (Derrick Smith), the Flyers sent Greg Adams, Ken Linseman, and a 1983 first-round draft pick (David Jensen) to Hartford. Howe went on to have a great career with the Flyers, setting club records for defensemen with 138 goals, 342 assists, and 480 points.

Rod Brind'Amour was acquired from the St. Louis Blues along with Dan Quinn on September 22, 1991, twelve days before the season opener, for Ron Sutter and Murray Baron. In his first season in Philadelphia, the center led the team in goals (33), assists (44) and points (77). Brind'Amour played eight full seasons with the Flyers, but, on January 23, 2000, he was sent to Carolina along with Jean-Marc Pelletier and a second-round draft pick for Keith Primeau and a fifth-round 2000 draft pick. He played 10 years with Hurricanes and 20 years overall in the National Hockey League. He was inducted into the Flyers Hall of Fame in 2015. Brind'Amour is 10th in club history with 235 goals, eighth in assists with 366, and his 601 points is 10th highest.

Mark Recchi spent two tours with the Flyers. On February 9, 1992, the right wing was traded by the Penguins to Flyers along with Brian Benning and Los Angeles's 1992 first-round draft pick (Jason Bowen) for Kjell Samuelsson, Ken Wregget, Rick Tocchet, and a third-round draft pick (Dave Roche). He was sent to Montreal on February 9, 1995 along with a third-round pick (Martin Hohenberger) in that year's draft for Eric Desjardins, Gilbert Dionne, and John LeClair. On March 10, 1999, the Canadiens traded Recchi back to the Flyers for Dainius Zubrus and two draft picks. In his two tours with the Flyers, he finished with 627 points, ninth best in Flyers' history. Recchi spent 22 seasons in the NHL and was one of a handful of players that played in four decades. He was inducted into the Hockey Hall of Fame in 2017.

John LeClair was acquired when the Flyers traded Mark Recchi to Montreal. LeClair spent 10 years in Philadelphia and the left wing led the club in goals scored five straight years beginning with the 1995–96 season, a Flyers record. He scored

50 or more goals three straight times starting in 1995–96. LeClair played on one of the top lines in Flyers history, "The Legion of Doom" with Mikael Renberg and Eric Lindros. LeClair scored 333 goals with the Flyers, fifth best in team history, and is eighth in points with 643. When the new Collective Bargaining Agreement went into effect on July 22, 2005, the Flyers had to part ways with LeClair to make room for cap space. He was inducted into the Flyers Hall of Fame in 2014.

10 California Seals.

Philadelphia fans had to wait a week to see the Flyers play at the Spectrum. No one knew how good they were going to be. Schedule makers had the Flyers open on the road on the West Coast and they would work their way back East with two more road games. The Flyers lost their first game, 5–1, to the Seals in Oakland. Bill Sutherland scored the first goal in Flyers history to tie the game, 1–1. Leon Rochefort and John Misuk recorded the team's first assists. The Seals came back and scored four straight goals, two in the second period and two in the third period. The first penalties of the game were called after only 21 seconds. Lou Angotti took the first Flyers penalty for interference while Larry Cahan of the Seals got whistled for slashing. Bernie Parent suffered the first loss. Next, the Flyers dropped a 4–2 decision to the Kings in Los Angeles. The expansion era was underway in the National Hockey League.

11 St. Louis Blues.

The Flyers headed to St. Louis after dropping their first two games on the West Coast. The city was still excited by the Cardinals winning their eighth World Series after beating the Boston Red Sox in seven games. St. Louis got an NFL team in 1960 from Chicago but had yet to win a championship. The Hawks were already established in the NBA, making it to the NBA finals four times and winning the title in 1958. For the first time, St. Louis was represented by four sports teams, but it lasted one year as the Hawks were sold and moved to Atlanta. The Flyers beat the Blues, 2–1, but at the end of the season, St. Louis made it to the finals and lost to Montreal in four straight. The Blues had changed coaches after only 16 games, firing Lynn Patrick who got off to a 4–10–2 start, and hiring Scotty Bowman. Bowman turned things around as the Blues went 23–21–14 under the future Hall of Fame coach. The Blues finished third in the regular season and beat the Flyers, who finished first in the regular season, in seven games. Also making the playoffs was Los Angeles which finished second, and Minnesota, which came in fourth. After a scoreless first period, the Blues scored early in the second before the Flyers tied the game on a goal by Lou Angotti in the final minute of the period. Ed Hoekstra scored the game-winning goal at 12:20 in the third period as Doug Favell became the first Flyers goalie to win a game.

12 Pittsburgh Penguins.

The Flyers drew one of the expansion teams for their first game in the Spectrum. The building was only half full. The team had gotten off to a 1–2 start. Not only was the team new, so was their opponent and not many people knew who the Flyers players were much less those for Pittsburgh. Hopefully, a rivalry would start with these two teams from Pennsylvania. Up until this time, the Phillies had yet to win a World Series while the Pirates had won three. The Phillies and Pirates were meeting 18 times a year and the Eagles and Steelers had been going at it every year since 1933, most of the times twice. At the time, the Eagles had won three NFL championships and the Steelers none. The days and nights of consistent Flyers sell-outs was still about two years away. Getting to the sports complex, which was starting to get built up wasn't easy. The Girard Point Bridge on I-95 wasn't completed yet. The subway ended at Snyder Avenue, 15 blocks from the Spectrum. Both opened in 1973, two years after Veterans Stadium did. One thing that favored the Flyers was that there was plenty of parking.

Game time was set for 8 p.m. NHL President Clarence Campbell was on hand to drop the first puck. The game was scoreless until the third period when Ed Hoekstra fired a shot from the blue line, but Penguins goalie Les Binkley blocked the shot. The puck bounced in front of him and Bill Sutherland pounced on it and put it into the net with 2:59 gone in the third period for the only goal of the game, one of only 17 shots the Flyers took all night. Leon Rochefort and Hoekstra picked up the assists. Playing strong defense throughout, the Flyers limited Pittsburgh to just three shots on goal in the third period.

13 Doug Favell.

Doug Favell posted the first shutout in Flyers history when they won their first game at the Spectrum, 1–0. This was only the team's fourth game and Favell got the nod over Bernie Parent, who started the first game of the season in Oakland. Favell started his third straight game and he stopped all 17 shots that evening. It was the first of Favell's four shutouts that season. He also posted the first Flyers shutout on the road when he blanked the Los Angeles Kings, 3–0.

Favell would spend six seasons with the Flyers and divide his time over his six final seasons between Toronto and the Colorado Rockies. He was traded to the Maple Leafs in a deal that bought Bernie Parent back to the Flyers. Parent had been traded to Toronto in 1970–71. Favell had carried the Flyers to their first winning season in his final year in Philadelphia and helped the Flyers win their first playoff series over Minnesota in 1972–73 before falling to the eventual Stanley Cup champion Montreal Canadiens in five games. As much as Favell had played some terrific hockey that season, he wasn't as consistent as the Flyers would have liked. Keith Allen knew that getting Parent back might make a big difference in the Flyers' bid to win their first Stanley Cup championship.

14 Detroit Red Wings.

Not only were Flyers fans going to see one of the established teams, they were getting their first look at Gordie Howe, considered by many to be the greatest player in the history of the NHL. He finished his career holding the record for scoring the most goals with 801, which held up until surpassed by Wayne Gretzky. The Red Wings won the game, 3–1, as Ted Hampson and Paul Henderson turned the red light on for Detroit in the first period. Gary Dornhoefer scored with 50 seconds gone in the second period but, with only 28 seconds to go before the second intermission, Doug Roberts got the Red Wings back to a two-goal lead. Detroit outshot the Flyers, 36–21. The Flyers drew a crowd of 10,859, their first crowd over 10,000 but still short of a sellout. It was obvious that the established teams would draw a crowd. The next two opponents at the Spectrum were the Seals and the North Stars and less than 5,000 were at each game. Montreal was the next Original Six team to visit to Philadelphia, drawing 9,188.

15 Montreal Canadiens.

The Flyers' first win against an established team was over the Montreal Canadiens in the Forum. The Canadiens had won the Stanley Cup in 1965 and 1966 before being dethroned by Toronto in the last season before expansion. Bernie Parent, who was born and raised in Montreal, got the start while Rogie Vachon started in goal for the Canadiens. It was all Flyers as they never trailed in the game. Leon Rochefort scored at 4:23 of the first period and Garry Peters scored with 1:48 to go before the first intermission. Montreal cut the lead in half on a goal by Gilles Tremblay at 7:28 of the second, but Rochefort came back and scored twice in the third period at 10:18 and 13:31 to become the first Flyer to score a hat trick. It was Parent's first win as a Flyer as the Canadiens outshot the Flyers, 34–19. The win showed that the Flyers could stay competitive against the established teams and weren't going to be embarrassed.

The following night, the two teams met at the Spectrum and tied, 1–1. Parent was back in goal, but Montreal went with Gump Worsley. Ed Hoekstra scored for the Flyers in the second period and Yvan Cournoyer matched that for Montreal in the third period. Once again, the Flyers were outshot, 31–23.

16 Lou Angotti.

Lou Angotti was selected as the Flyers' first captain right before the start of the season. The center had been taken in the expansion draft from Chicago, where he played the previous two seasons. Prior to playing in the Windy City, he started his NHL career with the New York Rangers, beginning in 1964–65 but during the next season he was traded to the Black Hawks. Angotti had his best season in the NHL with the Flyers, scoring 12 goals and adding 37 assists. He was sent to Pittsburgh the following year and played one year with the Penguins. From there, it was back to the Black Hawks for four years. Chicago went to the Stanley Cup Finals but fell to Montreal in seven games in 1971. Angotti finished his NHL career in St. Louis in 1973–74. After 55 games, he became their coach for the balance of the year. He started out the next season behind the Blues bench but, after the team started 2–5–2, Angotti got the pink slip. Nine seasons later, he was the coach of Pittsburgh but lasted only one year.

Although Angotti played only the inaugural season with the Flyers, he played a big part of the club finishing in first place in the West Division.

17 Toronto Maple Leafs.

The defending NHL champions when the Flyers joined the National Hockey League were the Toronto Maple Leafs.

Not only had they won it all in 1967, Toronto had previously captured three straight Stanley Cups beginning in 1962. Their streak was stopped in 1965 by Montreal, which won again in 1966. Since expansion, the Maple Leafs have failed to win another Cup, yet they are second with the most championships with 13 while Montreal still leads with 24.

The Flyers were 8–15–1 against the established teams in their first season including beating the Maple Leafs in three their four meetings. They were able to beat the other five teams once, beginning with road wins in Montreal and Boston, and the Flyers posted home wins against New York and Detroit. After beating Toronto on the road, the Flyers beat Chicago and Toronto at the Spectrum. Beating the Bruins and the Canadiens at home would have to wait another year. The Flyers' first road win in New York came the following season and their first win in Detroit took place during the 1969–70 season. Chicago fans didn't see the Flyers beat the Black Hawks in Chicago Stadium until the teams met for the second time in 1972–73 as the Flyers won it, 3–2. Up until that game, the Flyers were 0–10–5 in Chicago.

The last Original Six team the Flyers faced was Toronto and the Flyers skated away with a 2–1 win in Maple Leaf Gardens. Ed Hoekstra scored in the first period and Claude Laforge's goal in the third period offset a second-period Maple Leafs goal as Doug Favell stopped 46 shots. The next time these two teams met was at the Spectrum as the Flyers won it, 4–1, on a weekend where they posted consecutive wins over Chicago on Saturday and Toronto on Sunday before two sold-out crowds. John Miszuk scored twice in the first period while Laforge scored in the second and Don Blackburn turned on the red light on in the third period. Once again, Favell was in goal and stopped 43 shots.

It was back to Toronto for the third meeting, but the Maple Leafs skated away with an easy 7–2 win. The final game took place in Quebec when the Flyers had to abandon the Spectrum due to problems with the roof and they beat the Maple Leafs, 7–4, as seven different players scored goals for the Flyers. Parent was the winning goalie, stopping 44 shots.

18 Bill Clement.

Keith Allen was hired by the Flyers' first general manger, Bud Poile, to be the team's first coach. Allen stayed behind the bench for the first two seasons, leading the team to a first-place finish in the West Division the first year. They lost to the St. Louis Blues in the first round of the playoffs in seven games. The following season, the Flyers struggled for most of the year and it appeared they might not make the playoffs, but in the final month of the season, they went 7–2–5 and finished in third place. One of the biggest factors in possibly

Keith Allen as coach, before becoming assistant general manager and later general manager.

going backwards was they played the Original Six teams six times instead of four and were 6–19–11 in those games while they were 14–16–10 against teams in their own division. The third-place finish matched them up with the Blues, who finished first and had been playing more experienced and bigger players. It was no contest as the Blues prevailed in four straight.

At the end of the season, Allen was named the assistant general manager and Vic Stasiuk, who coached the Flyers' top farm team in Quebec took over behind the bench. He had led the Aces to the finals twice, losing to Rochester in six games and Hershey in five games. Right before Christmas, Ed Snider fired Poile and Allen became the general manger. It was Keith's turn to call the shots and when the Flyers made their first selection in the 1971 draft, they took center Bill Clement who debuted with the Flyers in 1971–72 and was with the team through 1975. After winning the Stanley Cup for the second straight year, Clement was traded with Don McLean and the Flyers' first-round draft pick to the Washington Capitals for the first overall pick in the draft, which they used to select Mel Bridgman.

Allen's second pick in 1971 was Bob Kelly, who, along with Clement, played a big part in the Flyers winning two Stanley Cups.

19 St. Louis Blues.

Bernie Parent's first shutout with the Flyers came against St. Louis at the Spectrum, 1–0, on December 16, 1967. Lou Angotti scored the only goal with 56 seconds left in the second period. Parent stopped 25 shots while Glenn Hall of the Blues stopped 16 of 17 shots. Parent would go onto set the Flyers' record for the most career shutouts with 50. He led the league in shutouts three times, recording 12 each in the 1973–74 and 1974–75 seasons and, in his last full season in 1977–78, had seven. Parent suffered a career-ending eye injury in 1978–79 season and finished the season with four shutouts, one less then Ken Dryden, who led the league with five.

20 Paul Holmgren, Terry Simpson, Wayne Cashman, Craig Ramsey, Bill Barber, John Stevens, and Craig Berube.

Paul Holmgren took over as coach for Mike Keenan, who was fired after four seasons. Keenan took the Flyers to the Stanley Cup finals twice. Holmgren had been hired as an assistant coach in the 1985–86 season. When he took over at the start of the 1988–89 season, he was the seventh coach in club history, but the first to win in his coaching debut. The Flyers opened the season against the New Jersey Devils at the Spectrum and skated away with a 4–1 win. The Flyers were trailing, 1–0, in the first period when Rick Tocchet tied it up. Goals by Scott Mellanby and Derrick Smith put Flyers ahead for good in the second period and Murray Craven closed out the scoring with a third-period goal. Ron Hextall was in goal and had 32 saves.

Terry Simpson was the ninth coach in team history and the second to win his first game behind the bench. He was also the first Flyers coach who had been a head coach in the NHL before coming to Philadelphia. In his first game, the Flyers had to come from behind to beat the Penguins, 4–3, at the Spectrum. The Flyers were down, 2–0, in the first period but goals by Rod Brind'Amour and Eric Lindros tied it up. The teams swapped goals in the second period before Dmitry Yushkevich scored the game-winning goal at 7:47 in the third period. Dominic Roussel picked up the win for the Flyers.

Despite taking the Flyers to the Stanley Cup Finals in 1996–97 where they lost to Detroit in four straight, Terry Murray was let go by the Flyers at the end of the season and Wayne Cashman was named the new coach, the 11th in team history. Cashman's tenure lasted 61 games, but in his first game, the Flyers beat Florida, 3–1, in the Core States Center (as the Wells Fargo Center was then known). The game was tied, 1–1, in the second period when goals by Dainius Zubrus and Pat Falloon won it for the Flyers with Ron Hextall in goal.

Craig Ramsay took over for Roger Neilson after 57 games of the 1999–2000 season after Neilson was diagnosed with bone cancer. Ramsay was the third coach in Flyers history to have been a head coach before taking over the Flyers, having coached Buffalo. The club's first game under Ramsay was against the Rangers in Madison Square Garden. John Vanbiesbrouck gave Ramsay his first win as the Flyers came away with a 3–2 victory. New York had led, 2–1, after two periods but third-period goals by Mikael Renberg and John LeClair gave the Flyers the victory.

Bill Barber replaced Ramsey 28 games into the 2000–01 season and the Flyers came away with a 5–2 win in the First Union Center (as the Wells Fargo Center was then known) over the New York Islanders. Down 1–0 in the first period, Keith Primeau tied the game with 1:22 to go in the period. Two quick goals in the second period—at 2:07 by Primeau and at 2:27 by Eric Desjardins—put the Flyers up, 3–1. The Islanders closed to within one by the end of the second period. Goals by Peter White and Kevin Stevens in the third period gave Barber a win in his first game behind the bench. Roman Cechmanek was in goal for the Flyers.

Ken Hitchcock, who replaced Barber, was let go only eight games into the 2006–07 season with a 1–6–1 record and was replaced by John Stevens. In his first game as coach, the Flyers came away with a 3–2 shootout victory over the Atlanta Thrashers. The teams traded goals in the first and third periods. Randy Robitaille scored in the first period to put the Flyers ahead, but Atlanta tied it before the first intermission. Peter Forsberg scored with 56 seconds gone into the third period, but the Thrashers tied the game at 8:31 to send it into overtime. Forsberg won it for the Flyers in the shootout and Antero Nittymaki was in goal for Philadelphia.

Peter Laviolette had started the 2013–14 season 0–3 when he was replaced by Craig Berube. This was the earliest change in coaches in Flyers history but not in Philadelphia sports. The Phillies still hold that distinction when Eddie Sawyer quit after the first game of the 1960 season and told everyone he was forty-nine and wanted to live to be fifty. (He lived to eighty-seven). The Flyers met Florida at the Wells Fargo Center in Berube's first game and beat the Panthers, 2–1. Brayden Schenn scored both goals for the Flyers in the first period and Steve Mason turned away 33 shots.

21 Paul Holmgren, Terry Murray, Bill Barber, John Stevens, and Craig Berube.

Paul Holmgren played 11 seasons in the National Hockey League. Before he joined the Flyers after being drafted in the sixth round in 1975 from the University of Minnesota, he played the 1975–76 season with the Minnesota Fighting Saints of the World Hockey Association. Holmgren, who was born in St. Paul, Minnesota, followed up and played six games with the Flyers' top farm team, the Richmond Robins in the American Hockey League and one game with the Flyers.

Holmgren has done it all for the Flyers, He has been a player, assistant coach, head coach, a scout, assistant general manager, general manager, and was named president of club in 2014. He played 500 games in Philadelphia and had 138 goals and 171 assists for 309 points and added 1,600 penalty minutes.

Terry Murray was the next former player to coach the Flyers. He not only played and coached the Flyers, he was also a scout, assistant coach, and a minor-league coach. He had three tours of duty in Philadelphia, playing in 115 games between 1975–76 and 1980–81. Murray turned to coaching starting with the Capitals but was let go during his fifth season there. He wasn't out of the NHL for long. Murray then coached the Flyers for three seasons, winning the Atlantic Division twice and in his third and final season, won the Eastern Conference championship and reached the Stanley Cup Finals. After winning the first three series in just 15 games by winning all three series in five games over Pittsburgh, Buffalo, and the New York Rangers, the Flyers were taken out by Detroit in four straight games in the Stanley Cup Finals. After losing Game Three, 6–1, in Detroit, Murray said in a meeting with his players that the Flyers were in a choking situation. After being swept, Murray was let go as coach and remained with the team the following season as a scout. His three-year record was 118–64–30. Murray later coached Florida and Los Angeles and, in between those two stints, returned to the Flyers, first as a scout and, then as an assistant coach. After the AHL Phantoms moved from the Spectrum to Adirondack, he coached the team for two years beginning in 2012–13. When the Phantoms moved to Allentown in 2014–15, Murray coached the team the first season.

Bill Barber was drafted in the first round in 1972. He began the 1972–73 season by playing 11 games with Richmond Robins, then was called up to the big club. In his rookie season, he scored 30 goals and picked up 34 assists, good for 64 points. Barber went onto to have a great career with the Flyers and was inducted into the Flyers Hall of Fame in the second class with Keith Allen and Ed Snider and was voted into the Hockey Hall of Fame in 1990. Barber is still the club leader in goals scored with 420, second in power play goals with 104, second in short-handed goals with 31, third in assists with 463, second in points with 883 and games played with 903. In 1975–76, Barber became the third Flyers player to score 50 or more goals in a season. He spent 11 seasons with the Flyers and scored 20 or more goals every year. He was selected to play in six All-Star Games and scored goals in the 1978 and 1981 contests. Barber made the NHL All-Star Team at left wing in 1975–76 and made the second team in 1978–79 and 1980–81. After undergoing knee surgery in the spring of 1984, he tried a comeback and couldn't make it, retired and turned to coaching. Barber was an assistant coach with the Flyers before he took the Phantoms to the Calder Cup title in 1998. Barber took over the Flyers during the 2000–01 season and brought the club home in second place and followed up by winning the Atlantic Division the next season. The Flyers were eliminated in the first round of the playoffs both times and Barber, who went 73–40–17 in the regular season, lost his job. Barber has since returned to the Flyers as a scouting consultant.

John Stevens's career with the Flyers totaled only nine games in the 1986–87 and 1987–88 seasons after he was taken in the third round of 1984 draft. Stevens later spent parts of three seasons with Hartford, but most of his career was spent in the American Hockey League. He was inducted into the AHL Hall of Fame in 2012. Stevens was the captain of the 1998 Calder Cup champion Phantoms. An eye injury a year later ended his playing career. He turned to coaching as an assistant to Bill Barber. When Barber took over the Flyers during the 2000–01 season, Stevens became the head coach of the Phantoms for six years, making it to the playoffs four times and winning the Calder Cup in 2005. Stevens was promoted to assistant coach of the Flyers in 2006–07 under Ken Hitchcock but Hitchcock was fired after eight games and Stevens became the head coach until he was replaced by Peter Laviolette 25 games into the 2009–10 season. He went 120–109–34 and made the playoffs twice. Stevens then joined Los Angeles and has been an assistant coach, associate coach, interim head coach between Terry Murray and Darryl Sutter, and was named the head coach on April 23, 2017.

Craig Berube was signed as a free agent by the Flyers and spent two tours of duty as a player. He was with the team for five years beginning in 1986–87 and he returned in 1998–99 for two more years. All told, he played in the NHL with four other teams before turning to coaching. Berube started out as a playing assistant coach of the Phantoms in 2003–04, then served as an assistant coach for the next two years. He became head coach of the Phantoms in 2006–07 but his tenure lasted six games. When Hitchcock was fired as coach of the Flyers and John Stevens became coach, Berube became the assistant coach with the Flyers. He returned to the Phantoms as coach the following season and was brought back as an assistant coach for the Flyers in 2008–09. Berube replaced Peter Laviolette as the coach of the Flyers after three games of the 2013–14 season. He coached them for two seasons and was fired after the 2014–15 season after compiling a 75–58–28 record.

22 Ed Snider, Bud Poile, and Keith Allen.

Ed Snider founded the Flyers in 1966 and was inducted into the Hockey Hall of Fame in 1988 and the Flyers Hall of Fame in 1989. Many predicted that the Flyers wouldn't make it in the NHL and would soon move to Baltimore. Philadelphia didn't have a good reputation for being a hockey town, but

Snider changed that. Beginning in their third year, the Flyers began selling out their home games and under Snider, the Flyers were the first expansion team to win the Stanley Cup in 1974 and they repeated in 1975. Six other times, the Flyers went to the Stanley Cup Finals. They were the only NHL team to beat the Soviet Red Army team in 1976. That year, the Flyers became only the third Philadelphia sports franchise to reach the finals three straight years. The A's won two World Series in 1929 and 1930 and lost in seven games to the St. Louis Cardinals in 1931. The Eagles fell to the Chicago Cardinals in the NFL championship game in 1947 but quickly rebounded and won the title in 1948 over the Cardinals and in 1949 defeated the Los Angeles Rams. He created the Ed Snider Youth Hockey Foundation in 2005, created Flyers Charities, and built the CoreStates Center (now known as the Wells Fargo Center), which opened in 1996.

Bud Poile was hired as the first general manager of the Flyers a year before the team even started playing. He had played in the NHL with all of the Original Six teams with the exception of Montreal and later was a coach in the Western Hockey League. Less than a week later, Poile hired Keith Allen to be the first coach of the Flyers. Along with Marcel Pelletier, who was involved with scouting, the three spent a year looking at players in other leagues. During the third season, Snider fired Poile and elevated Allen, who had been made assistant general manager, to general manager. Poile later became the general manager of the Vancouver Canucks when they started play in the National Hockey League. Later, he became the president of the Central Hockey League and the commissioner of the International Hockey League. The Norman R. "Bud" Poile Trophy is given to the American Hockey League team who has the best regular season record in the Western Conference. Poile was inducted into the Hockey Hall of Fame in 1990.

Keith Allen was the first Flyers coach and he coached the team two years and won the first West Division championship. Allen played parts of two seasons with the Detroit Red Wings and was on their Stanley Cup–winning team in 1954. After coaching the Flyers a second year, he became the assistant general manager prior to the 1969–70 season to Bud Poile. Right before Christmas, Poile was fired as general manager and Allen took over the reins. The Flyers missed the playoffs that year when they lost their final game of the season to Minnesota at the Spectrum, 1–0. After making the playoffs for the third time in their first four years, the Flyers missed again in 1971–72 when they lost their final game of the season by allowing a goal with four seconds to go in Buffalo. After that, the Flyers finished first six times, made it to the playoffs 12 straight years, won two Stanley Cups and lost two finals. The Flyers record with Allen as general manager was 563–323–194. He was inducted into the Hall of Fame in 1992.

23 Keith Allen, Fred Shero, Pat Quinn, and Roger Neilson.

Keith Allen was the coach for the first two years of the franchise and he became their assistant general manager the third year. During that season Allen was promoted to general manager after Bud Poile was fired. In his first year as coach, the Flyers clinched the first West Division championship with one game left in the season. Moving onto the first round of the playoffs, they fell to St. Louis in seven games despite having a 7–1–2 record against the Blues in regular season. The following season, the Flyers fell back to third place and were eliminated in four straight against St. Louis. After the season, Allen moved into the front office.

Fred Shero was the coach for seven years beginning in 1971–72. He posted six winning seasons, made six trips to the playoffs, finished first four times (all consecutive beginning in 1973–74) and, won two Stanley Cups. Going for their third straight Stanley Cup in 1976, the Flyers lost to Montreal, which won their first of four straight championships, in the finals. Shero posted one of the biggest wins in club and NHL history when the Flyers defeated the Red Army team in 1976 in the final game of a series with the Soviet Union, which had sent two teams, with the Red Army squad having won two games and tied one. With the prestige of the league at stake, the Flyers won it with ease, 4–1. Shero had scouted the Russians' style of play and knew how to play against it. He left after the 1977–78 season and joined the New York Rangers, where he had earlier coached in their farm system, for three years. Shero took the Rangers to the Stanley Cup Finals in his first year on Broadway before losing to Montreal. "The Fog" was inducted into the Flyers' Hall of Fame class in 1990 but it wasn't until 2013 that he was finally inducted into the Hockey Hall of Fame, twenty-two years after he had retired from coaching. Shero's son Ray was the general manager of the Pittsburgh Penguins when they won the 2009 Stanley Cup and on May 4, 2015, was named the general manager of the New Jersey Devils.

Pat Quinn was inducted into the Hockey Hall of Fame in 2016. After the death of Barry Ashbee in 1977, Quinn was named his replacement as an assistant coach under Fred Shero, who left after the season. Quinn became head coach of the Maine Mariners of the American Hockey League, then took over for Bob McCammon during the 1978–79 season and, under Quinn, the Flyers went 18–8–4. He was behind the bench the following season when they had the 35-game unbeaten streak. The Flyers made it to the finals but lost to the New York Islanders in six games. Two of the defeats were in overtime including the final game when an earlier goal by the Islanders showed they were offsides. With eight games left in the 1981-82 season, the Flyers fired Quinn and bought back McCammon. Quinn later coached Los Angeles, Vancouver, Toronto, and Edmonton. He took Vancouver to the finals in 1994 but they lost to the New York Rangers in seven games.

Roger Neilson was only behind the Flyers' bench for two full years. He took over for Wayne Cashman on March 9, 1998, and guided the team to a second-place finish. After another second place finish the following season, the Flyers were in first place in 1999–2000 when Neilson had to step down as coach after 57 games when it was discovered he had cancer. He never returned to coach the Flyers. Neilson had started out coaching Toronto, Buffalo, Vancouver, Los Angeles, New York Rangers and Florida before coming to the Flyers. He finished his coaching career with Ottawa as an assistant coach, but, with two games left in the season, Jacques Martin turned over the reins to Neilson who coached the final two games, enabling Neilson to coach 1,000 games. Neilson was inducted into the Hall of Fame in 2002 and passed away a year later.

24 Mike Keenan.

Mike Keenan spent only one year with the Rangers, who went onto to win the 1994 Stanley Cup in seven games. Flyers fans could no longer chant, "1940" at the Rangers when they came to town. It took New York fifty-four years to win its fourth Stanley Cup after winning in 1928, 1933, and 1940.

New York defeated Vancouver, which was also coached by former Flyers coach Pat Quinn, in seven games. Keenan coached eight different teams, took five to the playoffs, and went to the finals twice with the Flyers and once with Chicago. Before coaching the Flyers, he won the Calder Cup championship with Rochester in 1983. Keenan also won the KHL Championship, the first non-Russian to win the title.

25 Bob McCammon, John Paddock, Bill Barber, and John Stevens.

Bob McCammon was the first to win the Calder Cup championship with a Flyers farm team, capturing it with the Maine Mariners in 1978 and 1979. McCammon replaced Fred Shero and coached the team for 50 games, compiling a record of 22–17–11 before being replaced by Pat Quinn. McCammon went back to Maine and won another Calder Cup. Both times, Maine took out the New Haven Nighthawks, first in 1978 in four games and in five games the following season.

John Paddock was behind the bench coaching Hershey when they won the Calder Cup championship in 1988 by sweeping the Fredericton Express. It was the Bears' seventh championship, but their first and only one as a farm team of the Flyers. The Bears became the first team to win three straight series in four games. First, they eliminated Binghamton and Adirondack. The Bears then turned the Express into the local and swept the series, outscoring Fredericton, 18–5. Paddock was inducted into the American Hockey League Hall of Fame in 2010.

The next future Flyers coach to win the Calder Cup championship was Bill Barber in 1998 with the Philadelphia Phantoms who defeated the St. John Flames in six games. The

Phantoms won the sixth and deciding game at the Spectrum which had the distinction of having both the Stanley Cup and Calder Cup championships clinched there. Barber, who was the Phantoms' first coach, was inducted into their Hall of Fame.

John Stevens was the fourth coach to win the Calder Cup championship with a Flyers farm club when the Phantoms defeated the Chicago Wolves in four straight in 2005. Stevens had been the captain of the Phantoms' first Calder Cup championship team, but an eye injury forced him to retire in 1999. He became an assistant coach with the Phantoms and eventually took over for Barber, who returned to the Flyers coaching staff in 2000–01. Stevens had scored the first goal in Phantoms history. On April 23, 2017, Stevens was named the coach of the Los Angeles Kings. He was voted into the American Hockey League Hall of Fame in 2012.

Four other future Flyers coaches won the Calder Cup championship before being the coach of the Flyers. Fred Shero was the first in 1969–70 with the Buffalo Bisons. Mike Keenan was next 13 years later with the Rochester Americans. Bill Dineen won two Calder Cup championships with the Adirondack Red Wings in 1986 and 1989 and the most recent was Peter Laviolette with the Providence Bruins in 1999.

SECOND PERIOD

The Flyers have had several great rivalries over the years. They had two right from the beginning with the St. Louis Blues and the Pittsburgh Penguins, who joined the NHL at the same time. The rivalry with the Blues was because of what was happening on the ice and the one with the Penguins was for state bragging rights. All three teams were in the West Division through the 1973–74 season. When the Flyers joined the NHL, it brought the league up to 12 teams, seven years later, the league had 18 teams split into two conferences, the Prince of Wales and the Clarence Campbell. Each conference had two divisions. St. Louis stayed in the same conference but not the same division with the Flyers while Pittsburgh switched conferences. The Flyers found themselves in the same division with the New York Rangers and the New York Islanders, setting up two new rivalries. The Boston Bruins became a fierce rival beginning in 1973–74. Later, the New Jersey Devils joined the mix with the Rangers and the Islanders.

(Answers begin on page 49)

1 What was the Flyers' record against the St. Louis Blues in their first season?

2 In the 10 games that the Flyers and Blues played that first year, how many times did the Flyers collect the most shots?

3 Flyers general manager Bud Poile once overheard something that the color commentator of the Blues said on the air during a broadcast from the Spectrum. He didn't like what he heard and confronted him. At whom was he yelling?

4 Who was the first Flyer to score a hat trick against the Blues?

5 What St. Louis Blues player scored six goals in a game against the Flyers at the Spectrum?

6 Beginning in 1968–69, the Flyers met St. Louis 28 times over the next four years. How many times did the Flyers beat them?

7 When Bernie Parent set the NHL record for the most wins (47) in a season by a goaltender, against what team did he have the most wins?

8 The Flyers were the first opponent in how many new NHL arenas?

9 What team was winless against the Flyers in the Spectrum in 42 games from February 7, 1974 to February 2, 1989?

10 Who was the first team the Flyers beat in overtime during the regular season?

11 The Flyers and Pittsburgh have met in the playoffs seven times. How many series have the Flyers won?

12 The Flyers beat the Penguins in Game Four of the 2000 Eastern Conference finals in five overtimes. Who scored the winning goal?

13 The best start in Flyers history was in 1986–87 when they won their first six contests. Who did they beat in the sixth game?

14 When the Flyers clinched the 1973–74 West Division championship, who did they beat and how many games were left in the regular season?

15 Which Original Six team did the Flyers play the longest before they won the season series from them?

16 After winning their first-ever game at the Boston Garden, how many years did it take for the Flyers to win their second regular season game there?

17 How many times did the Flyers and Bruins meet in the playoffs in the 1970s?

18 How many overtime games have the Flyers and Bruins played in the Stanley Cup playoffs?

19 What team did the Flyers beat to win their 500th game?

20 In the Flyers' third season, what team did they play six times with each contest ending up tied?

21 How many years did it take for the Flyers to win the season series from the New York Rangers?

22 What three former Flyers coaches coached the New York Rangers?

23 What former New York Rangers goaltender set the Flyers' record for the most consecutive shutouts?

24 The Flyers and Rangers have met in the playoffs 11 times. How many times did the Flyers win the series?

25 The Flyers swept all seven games from an opponent in a season three times. What teams did they sweep?

26 How many times have the Flyers and the Islanders met in the playoffs?

27 How many times have the Devils and Flyers met in the playoffs?

28 Since the 1982–83 season when the Devils moved from Denver to New Jersey and were placed in the same division as the Flyers, Rangers, and Islanders, how many times have the Flyers finished in first place?

29 What team did the Flyers beat for their 1,000th win?

30 Who holds the club record for the most points scored in a season and, when he broke the record, what team did he do it against?

31 Who was the only player in NHL history to score three short-handed goals while his team was down two men?

32 When the Flyers set the club record for the most short-handed goals in a game with three in 1996, what team did they score them against?

33 Who did the Flyers play in their first Winter Classic in 2010?

34 Who was the Flyers' opponent in the 2012 Winter Classic at Citizens Bank Park?

35 Two days before the Flyers played in the 2012 Winter Classic, the Flyers took on the alumni of another team. What team was it and who won the game?

SECOND PERIOD
ANSWERS

1 7–1–2.

The Flyers won their first four games against the Blues. St. Louis was the last of the six expansion teams to get into the NHL, but the first to have a coaching change. After a 4–10–2 start, general manager-coach Lynn Patrick turned the coaching duties over to Scotty Bowman. Patrick's teams lost their first two games against the Flyers and Bowman's team went 1–5–2. It wasn't until the ninth meeting that the Flyers lost to St. Louis. In goal, Bernie Parent was 4–0–2 while Doug Favell went 3–1. Parent got his first shutout in the NHL by blanking the Blues, 1–0, in St. Louis.

The Flyers won the first West Division championship by one point over Los Angeles and St. Louis was third, three points out of first place. The Flyers met the Blues in the first round of the playoffs and this was when the rivalry took off. The Blues were bigger, stronger, and more experienced with the Plager brothers (Barclay and Bob), Al Arbour, and Noel Picard. There were plenty of fights and St. Louis came away with the series in seven games after the Flyers tied the series by winning the sixth game in St. Louis in double overtime on Don Blackburn's goal at 11:18. Game Seven was back at the Spectrum and St. Louis had a secret weapon. The Blues' farm team in Kansas City under player-coach Doug Harvey had just been eliminated from the playoffs and Harvey, one of the NHL's all-time greatest defensemen, was called up and controlled the seventh game, with the Blues winning, 3–1.

2 One game.

The Flyers went more for defense than offense when putting their first team together.

In the first year, they were 11th in goals scored but third in fewest goals allowed. Leon Rochefort led the team in goals with 21 and Bill Sutherland had 20. Lou Angotti led the Flyers with 37 assists and 49 points. In their 10 meetings, the Flyers only outshot the Blues once, in the second game between the two teams and the first at the Spectrum. The Flyers took 29 shots while the Blues got off 15. In the third meeting between the two teams, the Flyers took only 23 shots while St. Louis fired 47 shots at Bernie Parent, but the Flyers hung on for a 2–1 win. In the 10 games, the Flyers took 252 shots on goal while St. Louis took 320.

3 Gus Kyle.

KMOX in St. Louis, a 50,000-watt radio station, carried the Blues games. Dan Kelly was their play-by-play announcer and Gus Kyle, who had spent three years as a player with the Rangers and Bruins, was doing the color. Flyers general manager Bud Poile was pacing back and forth behind writers and broadcasters in the press box when he heard Kyle say something that he didn't like. Instead of waiting for a break in the action, Poile snapped at him, "Why don't you tell the truth?" while the game was going on. Fans listening to game back in St. Louis were entertained by the shouting match. Poile never was one to hold back saying anything. When the Flyers got off to a slow start their second year, he stated that players were not concentrating on hockey because they were too busy taking their wives or girlfriends shopping or doing errands.

4 Don Saleski.

It wasn't until the 1977–78 season that a Flyer scored a hat trick against the Blues in the regular season. After the Flyers had gone 7–1–2 against St. Louis in the first year, the Blues dominated play for the next four years. The Flyers turned that around in 1972–73 and have dominated the series since, winning an average of three of every four games. In the first meeting between the teams in 1977–78 and the 65th overall, Don Saleski scored three goals as the Flyers beat the Blues, 7–0, at the Spectrum. Rick MacLeish scored the only goal in the first period, but Saleski scored two goals in the second period and before the period ended, Rick Lapointe, Bob Dailey, and Bill Barber scored, making it 6–0. Saleski got his third goal at 4:55 in the third period. It was Saleski's third and final hat trick of his career.

5 Red Berenson.

The Flyers and the Blues were meeting for the second time during the 1968–69 season, the first time at the Spectrum. Red Berenson scored six goals, one short of the NHL record as the Blues skated away with an 8–0 win. Not only did Berenson score six goals on 10 shots, he had never achieved a hat trick in the NHL while playing for the Canadiens or Rangers. This time, he doubled up. Berenson's six goals is still an NHL record for a visiting player. He scored his first goal in the opening period when he picked up a loose puck at the blue line, skated around Ed Van Impe and fired the puck over Doug Favell with a high shot into the left corner of the net. Berenson connected four times in the second period. After Terry Crisp, who would later play for the Flyers, and Camille Henry opened the third period with goals, Berenson scored his sixth goal. He was the sixth player to score six goals in a game, one short of the record set by Joe Malone of the Quebec Bulldogs against Toronto in 1920. St. Louis was still pushing the Flyers around and no one knew it, but Ed Snider told his front office personnel to get some tough guys. The groundwork would be put in motion at the end of the year for assembling the Broad Street Bullies and St. Louis quickly got the message they couldn't push the Flyers around anymore.

6 Four.

The Blues totally dominated the Flyers over the next four seasons as they beat Philadelphia 16 times in 28 meetings with eight ties. The Flyers only came away with four wins, but after that, it was all Flyers as they won the season series the next 11 years. In 50 games, the Flyers won 39, tied five, and lost only six, all in St. Louis. From 1971–72 through the 1987–88 season, the Flyers had an unbeaten streak of 34 games against the Blues at the Spectrum with 31 wins and three ties which included a 20-game winning streak.

7 St. Louis Blues.

Bernie Parent had six wins against the Blues in 1973–74 when he set the NHL record for the most wins in a season with 47. The record was later broken by Martin Brodeur of New Jersey with 48 in 2006–07, but that included wins in overtime. Parent still holds the record for the most wins in regulation. Parent beat all 15 opponents that season. He had five wins against Buffalo, Detroit, New York Islanders, and California. Parent beat Toronto four times, Minnesota and Pittsburgh three times, Chicago, Los Angeles, Montreal, and Vancouver twice, and Atlanta, Boston, and the New York Rangers once. Parent started the first 18 games of the season, got one game off, and then started 18 more in a row. He followed with streaks of four straight games and two straight games. After that, Parent started 28 in a row and after the Flyers clinched first place with four games left in the season, he started just two games. Bobby Taylor started the remaining games.

The Flyers tied Chicago for the fewest goals allowed with 164 as Parent shared the Vezina Trophy with Tony Esposito of the Black Hawks even though Parent averaged giving up 1.89 goals per game and Esposito gave up 2.05 goals per game. Parent led the league in shutouts with 12 and had 18 other games where he allowed only one goal. The following season, Parent had 44 wins. His longest consecutive playing streak was 20 games as Wayne Stephenson was the back-up for the most of that year.

8 Five.

With expansion coming in 1967–68, seven new buildings opened for the six expansion teams and one of the Original Six was getting ready to change playing sites. The Flyers opened four buildings on the road the first season. They played the first NHL game at Oakland-Alameda County Coliseum Arena but lost to the Seals, 5–1. Kent Douglas scored the first goal and the Flyers' first goal was scored by Bill Sutherland. Next, they played Los Angeles in Long Beach Arena, but lost to the Los Angeles Kings, 4–2. Sutherland scored the first NHL goal in that building.

The Kings were waiting for the Forum to be completed and when it was opened, the Flyers won the first game, 2–0. Ed Hoekstra and Leon Rochefort scored the goals and Doug Favell recorded the first shutout in the new arena. Later that season, the new Madison Square Garden in New York City opened above Penn Station on February 18, 1968, and the Flyers lost to Rangers, 3–1. Wayne Hicks of the Flyers scored the first goal at the new Garden. The next new building that the Flyers helped open was the Consol Energy Center (now known as PPG Paints Arena) in Pittsburgh in October 2010. The Flyers beat Pittsburgh, 3–2, as Danny Briere scored the first goal on a power play.

9 Pittsburgh Penguins.

The 42-game unbeaten streak began with the Penguins' final visit of the 1973–74 season. The Flyers were trailing, 4–3, in the third period but won it on goals by Bobby Clarke and Terry Crisp. During the streak, they beat Pittsburgh 39 times, including 23 straight and there were only three ties. The Flyers also shut out the Penguins five times, four by Bernie Parent and one by Wayne Stephenson. In Stephenson's shutout, the Flyers set the team record for the most goals scored in a shutout with 11.

Don Saleski picked up the Flyers' first hat trick in the undefeated streak on March 13, 1977, and Mel Bridgman got the next hat trick in the streak in 1981–82. Two years later, when the Flyers set the club record for the most goals scored in a game with 13, Brian Propp and Ilkka Sinisalo each had a hat trick and Dave Poulin recorded a hat trick against the Penguins in 1985–86.

When the Penguins finally broke the streak, they made it two in a row in the final two meetings of 1988-89, 5–3 and 6–5 in overtime, but before Pittsburgh got any ideas of building up a winning streak of their own in the Spectrum, the Flyers took care of the Penguins in the first meeting the following year, 4–1. The teams also met for the first time in the Stanley Cup playoffs in 1988–89 with the Flyers winning two of three in the Spectrum and the series in seven games.

10 Pittsburgh Penguins.

Bobby Clarke scored the winning goal at 2:43 of overtime against Pittsburgh on November 20, 1983. Bill Barber and Paul Holmgren picked up the assists. Overtime wasn't in effect when the Flyers joined the National Hockey League. Anytime you were trailing late in the third period and came back to score a goal to tie the game, you left the ice knowing you had picked up a point. Overtime went into effect in time for the 1983–84 season when the teams would play a five-minute extra period. If the game was still tied, it ended that way. Four years later,

any time a team lost in overtime, they were given a point. The shootout began in 2005–06.

The two teams were tied, 2–2, after the first period, but Mike Bullard put Pittsburgh ahead in the second period. The Flyers came back and scored twice to take a 4–3 lead on goals by Brian Propp, his second of the game, and Thomas Eriksson. There was only 5:08 to go in regulation when Bullard scored his second of the night to tie the game. The Flyers would play 14 overtime games their first year, winning three, tying 10, and losing one. Ilkka Sinisalo and Tim Kerr scored the goals in the next two overtime victories against Winnipeg in the Spectrum and against the Rangers in New York. The Flyers' lone OT loss came in Buffalo.

11 Four.

The Flyers and Pittsburgh have squared off seven times in the playoffs. The first time they met in the postseason was in the 1989 Patrick Division finals. The Penguins had home-ice advantage and the Flyers had to win the seventh and deciding game in Pittsburgh, 4–1. The Flyers never led in the series until the final game, winning the second, fourth, and sixth games. The Flyers went to the Wales Conference finals but lost to the Canadiens in six games.

The two teams didn't meet in the playoffs again until 1997 when the Flyers, who went to the Stanley Cup Finals before losing to Detroit, beat the Penguins in the Eastern Conference quarterfinals, 4–1. Three years later, the two teams squared off for the third time with the Flyers winning in six games in the Eastern Conference semifinals. The Flyers dropped the first two games at home but won the next two games at Pittsburgh in overtime, 4–3 and 2–1, in five overtimes. The Flyers closed out the series by winning the next two games, 6–3 and 2–1. The Flyers' season ended in the next round when they fell to the New Jersey Devils in seven games after winning three of the first four. New Jersey went onto to win the Stanley Cup.

It wasn't until eight years later that the Flyers and Pittsburgh met once again in the playoffs. The Penguins won the Eastern Conference finals in five games and went on to the finals where they lost to Detroit. It was the second time that they beat a team from Pennsylvania, as they defeated the Flyers 11 years earlier. The Flyers and Penguins met again in 2009 and Pittsburgh, who went onto win the Stanley Cup, took out the Flyers in the Eastern Conference quarterfinals, four games to two. The sixth time these two teams met in the playoffs was in the 2012 Eastern Conference quarterfinals with the Flyers prevailing in six games. Pittsburgh had home ice advantage, but the Flyers started off winning the first three games, two in Pittsburgh and wrapped up the series with an easy 5–1 win at the Wells Fargo Center after Pittsburgh won games four and five.

The two teams squared off for the seventh time in 2018 and Pittsburgh came away with the series in six games. The series started with the teams splitting the first two games in Pittsburgh. Coming back across the state, the Penguins won both games at the Wells Fargo Center. The Flyers forced a Game Six after winning the fifth game in Pittsburgh, but the Penguins wrapped up the series two days later in Philadelphia when they won the sixth game, 8–5, despite a hat trick by Sean Couturier.

12 Keith Primeau.

Keith Primeau scored the winning goal at 12:01 of the fifth overtime to win the fourth game of the 2000 Eastern Conference finals at Pittsburgh, giving the Flyers a 2–1 win. Dan McGillis and Luke Richardson assisted on the game-winner. The Flyers, who lost the first two games at home, won Game Three in Pittsburgh, 4–3, in overtime. The fourth game was the longest overtime game in the modern era in the NHL. Only a pair of playoff games in the 1930s went longer. The two teams played 152:01. The game took six hours and 56 minutes to complete. The Flyers set a club record by taking 72 shots while the Penguins took 58. Brian Boucher was in goal for Philadelphia. The team hopped their charter and landed at the Philadelphia International Airport as the sun was coming up.

The two teams caught a small break, having the next two days off before Game Five back at the Wachovia Center (as the Wells Fargo Center was then known). Boucher was back in goal for the Flyers. One player who wasn't affected by the long game was Andy Delmore, who became the only Flyers defensemen to score a hat trick in a playoff game, leading the Flyers to a 6–3 win in the fifth game at the Wachovia Center. The Flyers won the sixth game, 2–1, to clinch the series.

13 Pittsburgh.

The Flyers started off the 1986–87 season by winning their first six games. They opened their season with a 2–1 victory over Edmonton at the Spectrum in Ron Hextall's first NHL game. Goals by Ron Sutter and Peter Zezel won it for the Flyers. No one knew it at the time, but these same two teams would play each other in the final game of the season with the Oilers winning Game Seven of the Stanley Cup Finals.

The Flyers played their first road game two days later at Washington and beat the Capitals, 6–1. Returning home, the Flyers defeated Vancouver, 6–2, and then beat the Whalers in Hartford, 6–3. Back-to-back victories at the Spectrum over Winnipeg (3–1) and Pittsburgh (5–3) gave the Flyers their fifth and sixth straight wins. After a day off, the Penguins snapped the Flyers' six-game winning streak in Pittsburgh, 4–2.

14 Boston Bruins, 5–3, with four games left.

For the first six years after the NHL expanded from six to 12 teams, the new clubs played in the West Division. The Flyers won the West Division the first year, but St. Louis represented the West in the Stanley Cup finals each of the first three seasons. They were swept by Montreal in 1968 and

1969 and by Boston in 1970. The following season, Chicago switched from the East Division to the West and finished in first place three straight years until the Flyers dethroned them in 1973–74. By this time, it was apparent that the Flyers were the real deal. On March 30, 1974, they defeated Boston at Spectrum to capture the West Division title and they finished the season with 112 points. The Bruins won the East Division with 113 points.

The teams traded goals in the first period with Rick MacLeish and Ross Lonsberry scoring for the Flyers, but goals by Bill Flett and Bobby Clarke put the Flyers ahead for good, 4–2, in the second period. Lonsberry scored his second goal of the game in the third period before the Bruins came back with their third and final goal with 1:34 left. It was only the Flyers' fourth regular season home win over Boston in their first seven years, covering 38 games. There were four ties and 30 defeats.

15 Boston Bruins.

It wasn't until 1976–77 that the Flyers won the season series over the Bruins. They had won at least one season series against every opponent by the 1974–75 season with the exception of Boston. Against the five teams that joined the NHL at the same time as the Flyers, Philadelphia had won a season series against the five other expansion teams by 1969–70. It took until 1974–75 for the Flyers to win season series from Chicago, Detroit, Montreal, the New York Rangers, and Toronto from the original six. Boston had given the Flyers fits for years. Even today, the Flyers have a losing record both at home and on the road against Boston. In the first 46 games with Boston over the first nine years, the Flyers won six, lost 34, and skated to six ties, yet the first two times they met in the playoffs in 1974 and

1976, the Flyers won both series. When the Flyers finally won the season series for the first time in 1976–77, Boston knocked the Flyers out of the playoffs.

16 Nine years.

The first time the Flyers faced the Bruins in the Boston Garden, they came away with a 4–2 victory. The Flyers jumped out to a 1–0 lead when Joe Watson, who the Flyers took from Boston in the expansion draft, scored the first goal. Leon Rochefort and Bill Sutherland made it 3–0 at the end of two periods. Boston got two goals in the third to close to within one, but Don Blackburn scored an empty-net goal with 54 seconds left in the game. Bernie Parent, who was the first player the Flyers took in the expansion draft and had played for the Bruins, was in goal for the Flyers. No one knew it at the time, but it would take the Flyers another nine years to beat the Bruins in Boston during the regular season. In the next 22 meetings in the Boston Garden, the Flyers salvaged only four ties while losing 18 times. In that same period, the Flyers played the Bruins five times on the road in the playoffs and came away with three wins.

17 Four times.

The Flyers made it to the Stanley Cup Finals for the first time in 1974 and all that stood in their way of winning it all was the Bruins. Boston had won the Stanley Cup in 1970 and 1972 and were led by one of the greatest players of all time, Bobby Orr.

Boston had home-ice advantage and won Game One, but the Flyers came back to win Game Two on Bobby Clarke's overtime goal at 12:01 and they went on to capture the Stanley

Cup in six games. Two years later, the two teams met in the semi-finals and this time, the Flyers had home-ice advantage. After dropping Game One at the Spectrum, the Flyers took four straight. The rivalry continued for the next two years but Boston reversed the tables, taking out the Flyers in four games and five games.

The two teams met again in the playoffs in 2010 when the Flyers became the third NHL team and fourth overall in pro sports history to come back from a 0–3 deficit, winning Game Four in overtime at the Wachovia Center to start the comeback. The Flyers made it to the Stanley Cup Final but lost to Chicago in six games. A year later, the Bruins, still remembering what happened in 2010, swept the Flyers in the second round on their way to winning the Stanley Cup.

18 Eight.

The Flyers and Bruins have met in the playoffs six times and played 31 games with eight of them going to overtime. At least one game in each series went past 60 minutes. The most overtime games the Flyers have played against one team was against Buffalo but they met the Sabres in 50 games in nine playoff series. The first overtime game was in the Stanley Cup Finals in 1974 when the Flyers won Game Two at 12:01 on Bobby Clarke's goal. Two years later at the Spectrum, the Flyers won Game Two of the semi-finals when Reggie Leach fired the puck into the net at 13:38, giving the Flyers a 2–1 win.

The Bruins came back and won the next three overtime games beginning the following year. In the 1976–77 playoffs, the Flyers fell in four straight, losing Game One in overtime, 4–3. The Flyers had come back from a 3–0 deficit at the

Spectrum in the third period and tied the game on Clarke's second goal with 29 seconds to go but Rick Middleton won it in overtime at 2:57. Two days later, the Flyers fell in double overtime on home ice as Terry O'Reilly scored at 10:07 of the second overtime. The Flyers lost the next two games in Boston and were swept. A year later, Boston eliminated the Flyers in five games. The Flyers lost Game One in overtime in the Boston Garden, 5–4, on Middleton's goal at 1:43.

It was another 22 years before the Flyers and Bruins would meet in the playoffs. The Flyers had barely gotten into the playoffs, having to win their last game of the season in a shootout. They beat the New Jersey Devils in five games in the opening round. Meantime, the Bruins, who hadn't won the Stanley Cup since 1972, had started off by defeating Buffalo, also in six games, and took a quick 3–0 lead in Eastern Conference semi-finals against the Flyers. Boston won Game One in overtime on a goal by Marc Savard at 13:52 after the Flyers, who were down two goals in the third period, forced overtime on goals by Mike Richards and Danny Briere. In Game Four, the Flyers had taken a 4–3 lead when Ville Leino scored at 14:20 of the third period but former Flyer Mark Recchi tied it with 32 seconds to go in regulation. In overtime, Simon Gagne scored at 14:40, giving the Flyers the victory. They went onto win the series and became the third NHL team to come back from an 0–3 deficit. A year later, the Bruins took no chances with the Flyers, eliminating them in four straight games in the Eastern Conference semi-finals despite Philadelphia having home-ice advantage. The Bruins won Game Two at the Wells Fargo Center, 3–2, in overtime on David Krejci's goal at 14:00 and Boston went onto to win their sixth Stanley Cup.

19 Boston Bruins on November 2, 1980, at the Spectrum.

Bobby Clarke got the Flyers off to a 1–0 lead in the first period before the Bruins tied it. Rick MacLeish put the Flyers ahead in the second period before Boston came back and tied it, 2–2. Blake Wesley put the Flyers ahead for good at 14:44 of the second period. MacLeish got his second goal in the third period to seal the 4–2 victory.

20 New York Rangers.

The Flyers and Rangers met six times in 1969–70 with all six games ending in a deadlock. The two teams had also tied the final meeting between the teams in 1968–69. Bernie Parent was in net for all six games while Ed Giacomin played four games for the Rangers and Terry Sawchuk played the other two. In the first game at the Spectrum, the Flyers were trailing, 3–2, in the third period when Bobby Clarke scored for the Flyers. It was his first NHL goal as he put the puck past Giacomin at 16:36. Bill Sutherland and Wayne Hillman picked up the assists. The second meeting between the two teams was in Madison Square Garden and it was Jean-Guy Gendron that tied the game for the Flyers, 2–2, at 13:32 of the second period assisted by Andre Lacroix and Joe Watson. Giacomin was in goal once again for New York.

Their third meeting was also in New York and the Rangers came from behind to tie the game, 2–2, thanks to third period goals by Dave Balon at 1:14 and 16:40. The Rangers outshot the Flyers, 48–20. Once again, Giacomin was in goal for the Rangers. The next matchup was at the Spectrum and this time they tied, 4–4. The Flyers had taken the lead, 4–3, on a third-period goal by Dick Cherry at 5:06 but Arnie Brown tied it at 6:59. New York went with Sawchuk in goal. It was back to Madison Square Garden for the fifth game of the season series and this one ended, 3–3, with all the scoring coming in the first period. Earl Heiskala and Gary Dornhoefer staked the Flyers to a 2–0 lead but Jean Ratelle cut the lead in half. Garry Peters made it 3–1 for Flyers, but Balon got the Rangers back to within one and with 1:26 left in the period, Bill Farbairn tied it for New York. Parent had 38 saves while Sawchuk had 24.

The sixth and final meeting was at the Spectrum with Giacomin in goal for New York. Orland Kurtenbach scored for the Rangers at 2:45 of the third period, creating the sixth tie of the season. In each of the six games, the Rangers outshot the Flyers by a total of 220–165. In the first meeting the following season, the teams were tied, 1–1, at the Spectrum after two periods. Could there be an eighth straight tie between these two teams? That wasn't about to happen as Bob Kelly and Serge Bernier scored, making it a 3–1 final in favor of the Flyers.

21 Four.

The Flyers won the season series from the Broadway Blueshirts in only their fourth season in the NHL. The Rangers won three of four over the Flyers the first year and three of six the following season with two ties which became the rule in the 1969–70 season with six ties in six games.

At the time the Flyers joined the National Hockey League, the Phillies had been battling New York teams, the Giants since 1883 and the Brooklyn Dodgers since 1890 before they both headed west in 1958, but the New York Mets picked up the slack in 1962. The Eagles had been battling the New York Giants since 1933. Two Philadelphia teams, the Warriors (from 1946–47 to 1961–62 before they moved to San Francisco) and the 76ers (who moved from Syracuse to Philadelphia beginning in 1963–64) went at it against the Knicks. The Rangers had fallen on hard times after winning the Stanley Cup in 1940. They did make it to the finals in 1950, but that was it. It wasn't until their eighth season that the Flyers were in the same division as the Rangers.

The Flyers won the season series for the first time in 1970-71, winning all three games in the Spectrum. The Rangers won two in New York and the other game was a tie. The Flyers won their first season series over an established team in their first season by taking three of four from Toronto. The Flyers followed up and won over Detroit in 1974, Chicago and Montreal in 1975, and Boston in 1977.

22 Fred Shero, Roger Neilsen, and Mike Keenan.

Fred Shero had coached in the Rangers farm system for years until Keith Allen chose him to coach the Flyers. Shero had played parts of three seasons with the Rangers and then became a successful minor-league coach, winning two championships with the St. Paul Saints in 1960 and 1961 and the Calder Cup championship with Buffalo in the American Hockey League in 1970. Shero's final minor league championship came the following season with Omaha in the Central Hockey League before he took over the Flyers in 1971–72.

After seven years with the Flyers, Shero resigned and became the coach and general manager of the Rangers. The first season in New York was his best. The Rangers made it to the finals in 1979, knocking out the Flyers along the way. He got the Rangers back to playoffs the following year, but the Flyers returned the favor by eliminating them in the second round. After a 4–13–3 start in 1980–81, Shero was fired.

Roger Neilsen was the only one of the three that coached in New York before coming to the Flyers. Neilsen coached the Rangers for three-plus years before he was fired. He led them to first-place finishes twice, including 1991–92, when the Rangers finished with the most points, but halfway through the following year, Neilsen got his walking papers.

Mike Keenan was with the Rangers for only the 1993–94 season, but he ended the Rangers' 54-year championship drought. They broke the club record for the most wins in a season with 52, a record that held up for 21 years, and the Rangers won the Stanley Cup in seven games over Vancouver. Keenan has coached eight teams and took three to the Stanley Cup Finals. He later won the Kontinental Hockey League championship with Metallurg Magnitogorsk. Shero and Neilsen are in the Hall of Fame.

23 John Vanbiesbrouck with three straight shutouts.

John Vanbiesbrouck had been drafted by the New York Rangers in 1981 and played 11 years in the Big Apple beginning in 1981–82. He was taken by Florida in the 1993 expansion draft and after five years with the Panthers, was signed by the Flyers in 1998. He made his debut with the Flyers on the opening night of the 1998–99 season and shut out his former team, 1–0, in Madison Square Garden. The following season, Vanbiesbrouck had been in goal from the start of the season and the Flyers got off to a 1–4–1–1 start when he started his streak of three straight shutouts to set the club record for the most consecutive shutouts. In his last outing before the streak, in the Flyers' first win of the season over Buffalo, he gave up his last goal with 5:33 gone in the second period as the Flyers beat the Sabres, 5–2, at the First Union Center.

Three days later, the Rangers came to town and Vanbiesbrouck started his streak of three straight shutouts, 5–0, with 34 saves. Eric Desjardins put the Flyers up, 1–0, in the first period. Goals by Valeri Zelepukin and Mark Recchi in the second period and Jody Hull and Simon Gagne rounded out the scoring. Two days later, the teams met in Madison Square Garden and Vanbiesbrouck made it two straight shutouts, stopping 20 shots on goal. Daymond Langkow and Dan McGillis scored in the second period to give the Flyers a 2–0 win. Shutout number three in a row was back at the First Union Center and this one came against his other former team, the Panthers. Goals by Hull in the first period and by Eric Lindros in the third made it a 2–0 Flyers win as Vanbiesbrouck stopped 22 shots.

His streak ended in the next game at 13:13 in the first period as the Flyers lost to Vancouver at the First Union Center. Overall, Vanbiesbrouck went 227:40 without giving up a goal. After only two seasons with the Flyers, he spent his last two years with the Islanders and Devils and was inducted the United States Hockey Hall of Fame in 2007.

24 Six times.

The Flyers and the Rangers have met 11 times in the playoffs and Philadelphia has won six of them. The Flyers also have won the most games, 30–24. These two teams met for the first time in 1974 in the semi-finals and Philadelphia won the series in seven games. Bernie Parent hung up a shutout in the first game. The Flyers had won the West Division with 112 points while the Rangers finished third in the East Division behind Boston, which had the most points with 113, and Montreal. This was the last year where the West Division was made up of all the expansion teams and Chicago. The following season, the Rangers and Flyers were put in the same division. New York had been to the finals in 1972 but lost to Boston in six games. The Flyers and Rangers met for the second time in the playoffs five years later and Fred Shero in his first season coaching New York saw his team take out his former team in five games. The Flyers reversed the result a year later, taking out Shero's Rangers in five games. The Rangers got the best of the Flyers in 1982, 3–1, and swept the five-game Patrick Division semi-final series a year later.

The Flyers turned things around in the 1985 playoffs, defeating the Rangers in three straight games in the Patrick Division semi-finals. A year later, New York won the Patrick Division semi-finals in five, including the first and fifth games at the Spectrum. The division semi-finals became a best 4-of-7 in 1987, and the Flyers won it in six games as Ron Hextall turned in two shutouts. It wasn't until 1995 that the Flyers and Rangers met again, with the Flyers sweeping New York, 4–0, in the Eastern Conference semi-finals. Two years later, the Flyers eliminated the Rangers in the Eastern Conference finals in five games. This was the third straight series that the Flyers won in five games and it looked like they had a good shot at winning the Stanley Cup, but Detroit ended their bid when they swept the Flyers four straight even though Philadelphia had home-ice advantage.

It took another 17 years for the Flyers and Rangers to meet in the playoffs for the 11th time. New York had to go seven games to eliminate the Flyers and they did it by winning Games One, Three, Five, and Seven.

25 New Jersey Devils and Pittsburgh, 1983–84 and New York Rangers, 1984–85.

Only three times have the Flyers swept seven games from an opponent in the regular season. In 1983-84, they did it against both the Devils and the Penguins. The Flyers outscored New Jersey, 33–11. The closest they came to beating the Flyers was in the third game when they lost, 2–0. Bob Froese was in goal for the Flyers and New Jersey only got 15 shots on goal, while the Devils' Ron Low faced 44 shots. It was the second straight time that the Flyers shut out New Jersey. Pelle Lindbergh was in goal for the first shutout. Four of the games were at the Spectrum while the other three were in New Jersey. Three of the Flyers' final six regular-season games were against New Jersey over an 11-day span. The Flyers won, 4–3, in the Meadowlands, 4–1, at the Spectrum, and it was back up the turnpike for the final game with the Flyers skating away with a 6–2 victory.

Pittsburgh took the same punishment from the Flyers, losing all seven games. Three were in Philadelphia and four were in Pittsburgh. The Flyers outscored the Penguins, 46–21. The closest the Penguins came to defeating the Flyers was in the third game between the two teams, but the Flyers came away with a 5–4 overtime win for the Flyers' first overtime victory. Bobby Clarke scored the winning goal at 2:43. The worst loss for the Penguins was the Flyers' 13–4 win at the Spectrum. The Flyers were up, 6–4, heading into the third period before the Flyers scored seven straight goals.

Despite sweeping seven games from two opponents in 1983–84, the Flyers finished third in the Patrick Division, six points behind the first-place Islanders. The season came to a crushing halt when they were eliminated in the first round of the playoffs by Washington. Bob McCammon was let go as coach and general manager and replaced by Clarke, who hired Mike Keenan as the new coach.

Keenan's first team not only swept the Rangers in seven games in the regular season, they finished first in the Patrick Division and led the NHL in points with 113.

The teams met four times in the Spectrum and three times in Madison Square Garden and the Flyers outscored the Rangers, 31–13. The Flyers had won the final two meetings the previous season, making it nine straight wins. Over the Flyers' final nine games of the season, they met New York three times. The Flyers continued their dominance of the Rangers in the playoffs, sweeping them in three games and then taking their first two meetings in 1985–86, making it 11 straight regular-season wins and 14 overall.

26 Four times.

The New York Islanders joined the National Hockey League in 1972–73 and two years later met the Flyers in the playoffs for the first time. The Flyers have won three of four series, but the Islanders won the most important series in the 1980 Stanley Cup Finals. The Islanders made it to the playoffs in their third year and in the best 2-of-3 preliminary round, beat the Rangers by taking the third and final game only 11 seconds into overtime at Madison Square Garden. The Islanders then made headlines when they won their second playoff series in seven games over the Penguins, becoming the second team to come back from a 3–0 deficit. The Flyers won the season series from the Islanders, 3–1–2. The Flyers jumped out to a quick 3–0 lead but in Game Four, things started backwards. With the score tied, 3–3, and time running out, Reggie Leach fired a shot into the Islanders net, but before the red light could go on, the blue light went on which meant, no goal. The Islanders came back and won the game as well as games five and six and right away, everyone was talking how they came back against Pittsburgh and could they do it again. Not this time. Kate Smith came back to sing "God Bless America" before the game and it was all Flyers as they won the game easily, 4–1.

The second time the teams met in the playoffs was in 1980 finals. The Islanders won Game One in overtime on a goal by Denis Potvin and led the series after five games, 3–2. Game Six was at the Nassau Coliseum and the Islanders won in overtime, 5–4, on a goal by Bob Nystrom at 7:11. The game should never have gone to overtime, however. Tied, 1–1, in the first period, the Islanders scored their second goal of the game but, unfortunately, linesman Leon Stickle missed an offsides and Duane Sutter followed with a goal. Brian Propp scored for the Flyers at 18:58 as the two teams went to the locker room with the score, 2–2. Mike Bossy and Nystrom scored in the second period, putting the Islanders up, 4–2, but the Flyers answered that in the third period with goals by Bob Dailey and John Paddock before Nystrom scored the game-winner as the Islanders won their first of four straight Stanley Cups.

Five years later, the Flyers and the Islanders met in the Patrick Division finals and it was all Philadelphia as they won the series in five games. In the fifth and deciding game, Pelle Lindbergh shut out New York, 1–0. The Islanders were trying to get back to the finals for the sixth year in a row. They had lost to Edmonton a year earlier after winning four straight Stanley Cups. Two years later, the Flyers defeated the Islanders in the Patrick Division finals, only this time they had to go seven games.

27 Six times.

The Flyers' rivalry with the Rangers started as soon as they joined the NHL. The Islanders came into the NHL in 1972-73 and within three years, had a big rivalry going with the Flyers beginning with the 1975 playoffs. The Flyers' first series against the Devils franchise was in 1978 when the team was known as Colorado Rockies and the Flyers beat them in the preliminary round, 2–0. The team moved to New Jersey in 1982–83.

Their first postseason meeting came in the 1995 Eastern Conference finals. Just qualifying for the playoffs that year was a big accomplishment. The Flyers had missed the playoffs the previous five years. They were knocked off in six games despite having home-ice advantage. New Jersey went on to beat

Detroit to win their first Stanley Cup. The two teams went at it five years later in the Eastern Conference finals. The Flyers led three games to one but lost the fifth game at the First Union Center. Eric Lindros came back to the team for the first time since March, but they lost to the Devils, 2–1, in the sixth game. Lindros suffered a concussion in Game Seven when he was hit by Scott Stevens and was done for the night and the Devils went onto win the game, 2–1, and followed up by beating Dallas to win their second Stanley Cup.

The Flyers turned the tables in 2004 and 2010 when they beat the Devils in the Eastern Conference quarterfinals, both times in five games. The teams met most recently in the 2012 Eastern Conference semifinals with the Devils winning the series in five games.

28 Sixteen times.

The Flyers have finished in first place 16 times in 50 seasons of play. The Flyers hung a banner for the first time after their first season in the NHL and finished in first place four consecutive seasons beginning in 1973–74. Since the Flyers joined the NHL, the Rangers have finished in first place only five times. The Islanders joined the NHL in 1972–73 and the Flyers have finished first 15 times to only six times for the Islanders since then. After the Devils moved from Colorado to New Jersey in 1982–83, they have finished in first place nine times while the Flyers did it 10 times.

29 New York Rangers.

With 999 victories in the record book, the Flyers set sail for win 1,000 when the Rangers visited the Spectrum on January 9, 1993. The Flyers jumped to a quick 3–0 lead in the first period on goals by Mark Recchi, Ric Nattress, and Pelle Eklund. New York came back with two goals in the second period before Nattress got his second goal of the game by the time the teams went to the locker room for the second intermission. The Rangers got a goal at 17:31 of the third period, but the Flyers hung on for a 4–3 win. The following night, the Flyers shut out Edmonton, 4–0, to start on the team's next 1,000 wins.

30 Mark Recchi with 123 points in 1992–93.

Bobby Clarke had set the club record for the most points scored in a season with 119 in 1975–76. Playing on a line known as the "Crazy Eights," Recchi (No. 8) playing with Eric Lindros (No. 88) and Brent Fedyk (No. 18) had tied Clarke's record against Toronto in Maple Leaf Gardens on April 10, 1993, when he picked up an assist along with Lindros on a goal by Pelle Eklund as the Flyers came away with a 4–0 win as Tommy Soderstrom recorded the shutout. Two days later, Recchi set the record when he and Eklund assisted on the only goal of the game by Greg Hawgood as the Flyers blanked the New York Rangers at the Spectrum. This time, Dominic Roussel hung up the shutout. Recchi got his final three points of the season at Buffalo when he scored a goal in the Flyers' 7–4 win and in the final game of the season when the Flyers beat the Whalers, 5–4, in Hartford, Recchi finished with a goal and an assist.

31 Mike Richards with three.

The Flyers were meeting the Rangers in Madison Square on February 15, 2009, when Mike Richards, with an assist from Braydon Coburn, scored at 1:18 of the second period, putting the Flyers up, 2–0. They went onto win the game, 5–2. It was the third time that Richards had scored while the Flyers were killing off a 5-on-3 penalty, setting the NHL record for the most in a career. Four days later, Richards scored a shorthanded goal for the second game in a row as the Flyers beat Buffalo, 6–3, at the Wachovia Center and, two days later, he scored while a man down for the third game in a row in a losing cause to become the first player to this accomplish this feat in over 10 years in a 5–4 loss to Pittsburgh at the Wachovia Center.

32 New York Islanders.

The Flyers, battling the Rangers for first place, traveled to Long Island on April 2, 1996. Calgary had set the NHL record five years earlier for the most short-handed goals in game with three. The Flyers and the Islanders were tied, 2–2, in the second period when back-to-back short-handed goals by Shjon Podein (unassisted) and Joel Otto at 11:08 and 12:17, put the Flyers up, 4–2. Rod Brind'Amour and Eric Desjardins assisted on Otto's goal. Otto opened the third period with a goal and Brind'Amour added the third short-handed goal as Desjardins and Trent Klatt picked up the assists. The Flyers won five of seven games in April and won the Atlantic Division by seven points over the Rangers and the Eastern Conference by one point over Pittsburgh.

33 Boston Bruins.

The Winter Classic games have not been friendly to the Flyers. They first appeared in one at Fenway Park in Boston in 2010. Hitting pucks off the Green Monster wouldn't help a team win this game. The Flyers fell to the Bruins, 2–1. Bobby Clarke represented the Flyers and Bobby Orr represented the Bruins in the ceremonial faceoff.

After a scoreless first period, Danny Syvret scored the Flyers' only goal at 4:42 of the second period, but former Flyer Mark Recchi tied it with 2:18 to go in regulation. The shots were even at 25 when Marco Sturm took the 51st shot of the game and put it into the net at 1:57 of overtime. This was the third Winter Classic but the first time the home team won.

34 New York Rangers.

Two years after the Flyers played in the Winter Classic in Boston, the game came to Philadelphia and the Flyers took on the Rangers at Citizens Bank Park. New York was in first place in the Atlantic Division and the Flyers were two points behind. There were 46,967 fans on hand to see New York win the game, 3–2. Brayden Schenn scored his first NHL goal and Claude Giroux gave the Flyers a 2–0 lead in the second period before the Rangers closed to within one on Michael Rupp's goal before the second intermission. The Rangers got two goals in the third for the win. Rupp got his second of the game at 2:41 and Brad Richards scored the game winner at 5:21. The Flyers got a chance to tie it with 19.6 seconds to go when they were awarded a penalty shot but Danny Briere was stopped by Henrik Lundqvist. The Flyers outshot New York, 36–33. Keeping the rink intact for another four days, the AHL staged a game with the Flyers' Adirondack Phantoms farm team taking on the Hershey Bears. The Phantoms won the game, 4–3, in overtime before 45,653 fans.

The Flyers did play a third game outdoors on February 25, 2017, but it wasn't considered a Winter Classic game when they lost to the Penguins in Pittsburgh, 4–2.

35 New York Rangers.

It was natural that if you would have an alumni classic with the Flyers taking on the alumni of another team, you would pick the Rangers. Through the 2017–18 season, the two teams met 293 times in the regular season and the Flyers have won 125 games, lost 122 in regulation, suffered nine overtime losses, and the two teams skated to 37 ties.

Bobby Clarke and Mark Messier were at center ice for the ceremonial faceoff as Ed Snider dropped the puck before a crowd of 45,808 at Citizens Bank Park. The biggest cheers went up for Bernie Parent who played the first five-and-a-half minutes of the game. The Flyers started the LCB line of Reggie Leach, Bobby Clarke, and Bill Barber. Mark Howe also started on defense. This was one of the last times that the retired numbers of Parent (1), Howe (2), Barber (7), and Clarke (16) would be seen on the ice. Seven former players that made the Hall of Fame started the game: Barber, Clarke, Howe, and Parent for Philadelphia and Messier, Mike Gartner, and Brian Leetch for the Rangers.

Goals by John LeClair and Shjon Podein gave the Flyers a 2–0 lead before the Rangers cut the lead in half. Howe got that back for the Flyers in the third period and they went onto beat the Rangers alumni, 3–1.

THIRD PERIOD

During their first 50 years, the Flyers have had many great players who hold club and NHL records. Bernie Parent and Bobby Clarke have set most of those records.

Some players didn't spend that much time in Philadelphia but managed to put their names in the club's record book. Some should not surprise you, but others will.

(Answers begin on page 85)

1 What team did Bernie Parent have the most wins against as a Flyer?

2 Of the eleven other teams that were in the league when Bernie Parent joined the Flyers, he shut out each one he faced in the Spectrum during the regular season except one. Which team was it?

3 How many shutouts have the Flyers posted in season openers?

4 How many 1–0 victories do the Flyers have in their history, and what goaltender has the most?

5 How many scoreless ties have the Flyers played?

6 Ron Hextall holds the club record for goalies with the most lifetime wins. What opponent did he beat the most times?

7 Who were the goaltenders who set the Flyers' team record for the most consecutive shutouts in a season in 1996–97?

8 Who was only Flyer to wear number 16 before Bobby Clarke?

9 Bobby Clarke was the first Flyers player to score 100 or more points in a season. How many players reached the 100-point plateau before Clarke did it in 1972–73?

10 Rick MacLeish became the first Flyer to score 50 or more goals in a season in 1972–73. How many players had scored 50 in a season before him?

11 When Reggie Leach set the club record by scoring 61 goals in 1975–76, which team did he score the most against?

12 Who scored the two quickest goals for the Flyers in a game?

13 Who scored the three quickest goals for the Flyers in a game?

14 Who scored the four quickest goals for the Flyers in a game?

15 Who scored the quickest goal from the start of a game for the Flyers?

16 Only once did the Flyers have two players score 50 or more goals in a season. Who were the two players and what year did it happen?

17 Who holds the club record for the most consecutive seasons scoring 40 or more goals?

18 Which Flyer holds the NHL record for the most power play goals in a season?

19 Who holds the club record for the most overtime goals in a season?

20 What Flyers player set the NHL record for the most points scored in his first NHL game?

21 What Flyer set the NHL record for the most points scored in a game by a defenseman?

22 Who holds the club record for the most assists in a game?

23 Only one Flyers player scored a hat trick on the opening game. Who was he?

24 Only six times have the Flyers had two players have a hat trick in the same game. Who were the first players and what player was involved in three of the six games?

25 Who holds the club record for the most hat tricks in a career?

26 Who holds the club record for the most short-handed goals in a career?

27 Who holds the club record for the most consecutive games played?

28 Bobby Clarke became the youngest captain in Flyers history in 1972–73. When he became a playing-assistant coach in 1979–80, he had to give up being captain. Who took his place?

29 At three different times after the Flyers began play, there were three other teams that played in Philadelphia. Who were they?

30 Match these Flyers with their nicknames

1. Eric Desjardins	a.	Hound
2. Ron Flockhart	b.	Ghost
3. Claude Giroux	c.	Simmer
4. Sean Gostisbehere	d.	Rico
5. Bob Kelly	e.	Riverton Rifle
6. Reggie Leach	f.	G
7. Dave Schultz	g.	Flocky Hockey
8. Wayne Simmonds	h.	The Hammer

THIRD PERIOD ANSWERS

1 St. Louis Blues with 20.

Bernie Parent beat the Blues 20 times, 11 at the Spectrum and nine in St. Louis. The most wins he had at the Spectrum against one team was Pittsburgh with 14 and the most games he won on the road was the nine in St. Louis. At the time the Flyers entered the NHL in 1967–68, Parent faced 11 different teams and by the time he retired, six more teams had joined the league. His first win for the Flyers came against the Canadiens in Montreal and his first win at the Spectrum was against St. Louis. Parent's final win came at the Spectrum over the Kings and in his final game he suffered a career-ending eye injury against the New York Rangers at home in 1979.

BERNIE PARENT'S WINS BY OPPONENT

	HOME	AWAY	TOTAL
St. Louis	11	9	20
Los Angeles	11	7	18
Pittsburgh	14	4	18
Oakland/Cleveland	12	9	18
Minnesota	12	5	17
Vancouver	9	7	16
Toronto	9	6	15
Detroit	9	5	14
Buffalo	9	4	13

New York Rangers	8	5	13
New York Islanders	8	4	12
Atlanta	8	3	11
Boston	7	3	10
Chicago	9	1	10
Kansas City/Colorado	6	4	10
Washington	5	2	7
Montreal	4	2	6
Total	151	80	231

2 Boston Bruins.

Parent shut out each of those teams in the Spectrum during the regular season except Boston, but the one time that he did shut out the Bruins, it came in one of the most important games in Flyers history, the deciding Game Six of the 1974 Stanley Cup Finals. Eight new teams were added later on and Parent shut out all but two of them on home ice, Cleveland and Vancouver. Parent collected 38 of his 50 shutouts at home.

BERNIE PARENT'S SHUTOUTS BY OPPONENT

	HOME	AWAY	TOTAL
Pittsburgh	7	2	9
St. Louis	3	3	6
Los Angeles	5	0	5
Minnesota	5	0	5
Oakland/Cleveland	1	3	4
Vancouver	0	3	3
New York Islanders	2	1	3

Atlanta	2	0	2
Chicago	2	0	2
Kansas City/Colorado	2	0	2
Montreal	1	1	2
New York Rangers	1	1	2
Toronto	2	0	2
Buffalo	1	0	1
Cleveland	0	1	1
Detroit	1	0	1
Washington	1	0	1
Total	36	14	50

3 Four times.

It wasn't until their seventh season that the Flyers had an opening night shutout and it came at the Spectrum against Toronto on October 11, 1973. Bernie Parent was back with the Flyers and there was a lot of pressure on him. Tending goal for the Maple Leafs was Doug Favell, who had been sent to Toronto to get Parent back. Favell had helped the Flyers get to the second round of the playoffs a year earlier. Kate Smith made her first appearance at the Spectrum to sing "God Bless America" in front of a sellout crowd. Terry Crisp got the Flyers' first goal of the game at 12:52 of the first period with assists to Bob Kelly and Don Saleski. Bill Barber picked up an insurance goal (the first of his career) in the third period at 14:28 as Barry Ashbee and Bobby Clarke picked up the assists. The Maple Leafs outshot the Flyers, 28–24. Proving that Keith Allen made the right move getting Parent back, he shut out the Islanders in the next game, 6–0, on Long Island.

John Vanbiesbrouck, making his debut with the Flyers, was the second goaltender in club history to post a shutout on opening night in 1998–99 and he did it in New York, stopping the Rangers, 1–0. Vanbiesbrouck had started his career with the Rangers and spent 11 years in New York and five years with Florida before signing with the Flyers as a free agent before the season. At 5:45 of the second period, Alexandre Daigle got the lone goal of the game with Mike Maneluk and Chris Gratton picking up the assists. Vanbiesbrouck stopped 20 shots while Mike Richter, who went to high school at Germantown Academy in Fort Washington, had 29 saves.

Jeff Hackett in 2003–04 was the third goalie with an opening night shutout as the Flyers blanked Buffalo, 2–0, at the Wachovia Center. Like Vanbiesbrouck, he was making his Flyers debut after playing with five other NHL teams. Scoreless after two periods, the Flyers got third-period goals from Mark Recchi at 1:01 and Michal Handzus at 6:09. Hackett,

who spent only one year with the Flyers, faced 17 shots from the Sabres.

The most recent goaltender to record a shutout opening night was Ray Emery in 2009–10 at Carolina. Emery was making his debut with the Flyers in his first of two tours with the team. He stopped 28 shots. Goals by Jeff Carter and Mike Richards at 0:22 and 0:47 were all the Flyers needed. Danny Briere and Scott Hartnell picked up the assists on Carter's goal and Simon Gagne and James van Riemsdyk added assists on Richards's goal.

4 Twenty-six by 16 different goaltenders.

Bernie Parent leads the way with five 1–0 shutouts while Antero Nittymaki had three. Doug Favell, Ron Hextall, Roman Cechmanek, and Ilya Bryzgalov each had two. Favell recorded the first 1–0 shutout for the Flyers and it came in the first game at the Spectrum in the fourth game of the year. Parent set the club record for the most 1–0 wins in a season with three in 1973–74. His first came at the Spectrum against Chicago, his second at St. Louis, and his third was at home against Atlanta. Parent's fifth 1–0 win came early in the 1976–77 season over Los Angeles at the Spectrum.

Nittymaki (2005–06) and Bryzgalov (2011–12) season are next behind Parent for the most 1–0 wins in a season with two. Nittymaki's first came in a shootout against Calgary at the Wachovia Center with Mike Richards scoring the lone goal. He got his second less than a month later at Boston on Jeff Carter's goal. Bryzgalov got his two 1–0 shutouts only six days apart at the Wells Fargo Center. The first came against Washington on a goal by Eric Wellwood and the second over the Maple Leafs in a shootout won by Claude Giroux's goal.

Only two players have scored the only goal for the Flyers two or more times in a 1–0 win. Brayden Schenn leads the way with three. Schenn scored the lone goal for the first time in 2013–14 with Ray Emery in goal at New Jersey. His second was against Florida at home two years later with Michal Neuvirth in goal. Schenn collected his third 1–0 game-winner in overtime in 2016–17 against the Red Wings in Detroit with Anthony Stolarz in goal. Ross Lonsberry did it twice, in 1973–74 against the Blues in St. Louis and in 1976–77 against the Kings in the Spectrum. Bernie Parent was in goal for both games.

GOALTENDERS 1–0 WINS
PLAYERS SCORING IN 1–0 WINS

5 Bernie Parent	3 Brayden Schenn
3 Antero Nittymaki	2 Ross Lonsberry
	1 Lou Angotti
2 Ilya Bryzgalov	Bill Barber
Roman Cechmanek	Jeff Carter
Doug Favell	Paul Coffey
Ron Hextall	Sean Couturier
	Alexandre Daigle
1 Ray Emery	Michael Del Zotto
Robert Esche	Mark Freer
Bob Froese	Simon Gagne
Darren Jensen	Claude Giroux
Steve Mason	Derian Hatcher
Petr Mrazek	Greg Hawgood
Michal Neuvirth	Jimmy Johnson
Dominic Roussel	Kent Manderville

Anthony Stolarz
John Vanbiesbrouck

Brad McCrimmon
Keith Primeau
Mike Richards
Don Saleski
Darryl Sittler
Bill Sutherland
Eric Wellwood

5 Eight.

Scoreless ties in the NHL were as rare as seeing a NASCAR driver lead every lap of a race. They have been extinct since the NHL instituted the shootout in 2005–06. The Flyers' first scoreless tie came in the first season against the Kings in Quebec, where the Flyers were playing their home games while repairs were being made to the roof at the Spectrum. A pair of future Hall of Fame goaltenders faced each other as Bernie Parent turned away 32 shots and Terry Sawchuk of the Kings stopped 20 shots on goal by the Flyers.

The next scoreless tie was at the Spectrum in the Flyers' sixth game of the 1969–70 season and it was their fourth tie of the new campaign. Parent was once again facing a future Hall of Fame goaltender, Jacques Plante. The Flyers outshot the Blues, 26–25.

The third scoreless tie took place a year later in Pittsburgh. Les Binkley was in goal for Pittsburgh and he turned away 24 shots. For the third time, Parent was in goal for the Flyers and he made 30 saves.

It was another ten seasons before the Flyers played another scoreless tie. The Flyers and the Rangers met in Madison Square Garden. Rick St. Croix was in goal for the Flyers while Steve Baker got the nod for New York. Once again, the Flyers' opponent got off more shots on goal, 36–26.

The Flyers' fifth scoreless tie was their second against the Penguins in Pittsburgh and it took place during the 1982–83 season. Pelle Lindbergh was in goal for the Flyers and he stopped 24 shots while his counterpart, Denis Herron, stopped 30. It was another 10 seasons before the Flyers were involved in a game where the red light never came on and it was also the first scoreless overtime game in club history. From here on, all scoreless ties went another five minutes. Tommy Soderstrom was in net when the Flyers met the Canadiens at the Spectrum and he stopped 23 shots while Andre Racicot made 26 saves for Montreal. The seventh scoreless tie in club history came in 2000–01 when the Flyers and Tampa Bay met at the First Union Center. Roman Cechmanek stopped 36 shots for the Flyers while Kevin Weekes turned away 27.

The final scoreless tie was at San Jose and Jeff Hackett was in goal for the Flyers and it was his second straight shutout to begin the 2003–04 season. The Flyers were outshot by San Jose, 27–26. Evgeni Nabokov was in goal for the Sharks.

6 Washington Capitals.

Ron Hextall beat the Capitals the most times (25) with 16 wins at home and nine on the road. Hextall came up to the Flyers in 1986–87 and promptly won the Vezina Trophy, played in the All Star Game, and won the Conn Smythe Trophy as the Most Valuable Player of the playoffs. Hextall spent six years with the Flyers before he was sent packing to Quebec in the blockbuster trade that brought Eric Lindros to Philadelphia. After being away two years, he came back to Philadelphia for five more seasons and set the club record for the most wins by a goalie with 240, 18 of them shutouts.

RON HEXTALL'S WINS BY OPPONENT

	HOME	AWAY	TOTAL
Washington	16	9	25
New York Islanders	12	7	19
Pittsburgh	14	4	18
Montreal	8	5	13
New York Rangers	7	6	13
New Jersey	8	4	12
Buffalo	7	4	11
Tampa Bay	6	5	11
Carolina/Hartford	7	3	10
Colorado/Quebec	7	3	10
Boston	7	2	9
Toronto	4	5	9
Minnesota	5	3	8
Winnipeg/Phoenix	3	5	8
St. Louis	2	6	8
Vancouver	4	4	8
Calgary	4	3	7
Ottawa	4	3	7
Chicago	4	2	6
Florida	2	4	6
Los Angeles	2	4	6
Edmonton	5	0	5
Detroit	3	1	4
San Jose	1	3	4
Anaheim	1	2	3
Total	143	97	240

7 Ron Hextall and Garth Snow with four.

Garth Snow was in goal when the Flyers traveled to Hartford and beat the Whalers, 4–0, on December 14, 1996. The two teams were meeting for the second time in 48 hours after the Flyers had beaten Hartford, 3–2, at the CoreStates Center. The Whalers had scored with 2:30 to go in the game with Ron Hextall in goal. Following Snow's shutout in Hartford, the Flyers beat Boston the following night back home, 6–0, with Hextall recording the shutout. After three days off, the Islanders paid a visit to Philadelphia and were shut out by Snow, 5–0. On December 21, Hextall was back in goal as the Flyers made it four straight shutouts with a 4–0 win over St. Louis at the CoreStates Center. Immediately after the game, the Flyers were airborne for Chicago to meet the Blackhawks, who scored at 2:38 of the first period. The teams went on to tie, 2–2. The Flyers had gone 265 minutes and eight seconds without allowing a goal, also a club record.

8 Claude LaForge.

Claude LaForge played parts of five seasons with Detroit after starting his NHL career by playing five games with Montreal in 1957–58. He was playing with Quebec when the Aces were purchased by the Flyers before they started play in the NHL. Wearing number 16, LaForge played 63 games with the Flyers in the club's inaugural season and only two the following year, spending most of his time back in Quebec.

9 Eight players.

Bobby Clarke was the ninth NHL player to score 100 or more points in a season but was the first from an expansion club. Those to reach 100 or more points in a season before

Clarke were John Bucyk, Phil Esposito, Ken Hodge, and Bobby Orr of Boston; Bobby Hull from Chicago, Gordie Howe of Detroit, and Vic Hadfield and Jean Ratelle with the New York Rangers. No one from Montreal or Toronto had yet to score 100 or more points in a season, but at the same time, they were first and second in Stanley Cup championships.

Clarke picked up his 100th point of the 1972–73 season when he scored a goal in a 4–2 win over the Atlanta Flames on March 29. Three days later in the final game of the season, Rick MacLeish became the second Flyers player to reach 100 points in a season with a goal in a losing cause at Pittsburgh.

The Flyers were the third team to have two or more players score 100 or more points in a season. Boston was the first two years earlier when Bucyk, Esposito, Hodge, and Orr did it followed by the Rangers a year later with Hadfield and Ratelle.

10 Seven players.

Rick MacLeish was the eighth player in the National Hockey League to score 50 or more goals in a season. His 50th goal came in a losing cause as the Flyers fell to the Penguins in Pittsburgh, 5–4, on April 1, 1973. Maurice Richard and Bernie Geoffrion of Montreal were the first two players to score 50 goals or more in a season. Next was Bobby Hull of Chicago followed by Phil Esposito and John Bucyk of Boston. Vic Hadfield of the Rangers was the sixth and Mickey Redmond of Detroit was the seventh and he beat MacLeish to the 50-goal mark only five days earlier. MacLeish's club record for the most goals scored in a season held up only three years when Reggie Leach scored 61. It was MacLeish's only 50-goal season. The closest he came after that was four years later when he scored 49.

11 Atlanta Flames with 10.

Reggie Leach scored 10 of his club-record 61 goals in 1975-76 against the Flames, who entered the NHL in 1972–73. After eight years in Atlanta, they moved north to Canada, setting up shop in Calgary. Despite scoring 61 goals, Leach only had one hat trick and it came against the Flames at the Spectrum. Leach scored 28 goals at home and 33 on the road and recorded one or more goals against all 20 opponents. He scored against 12 different teams at the Spectrum and 15 away from home. At the time, he was only the second player to score 60 or more goals in a season. Phil Esposito of Boston did it four times.

REGGIE LEACH'S GOALS AGAINST EACH OPPONENT IN 1975–76

	HOME	AWAY	TOTAL
Atlanta	7	3	10
Minnesota	3	2	5
New York Rangers	2	3	5
Pittsburgh	2	3	5
St. Louis	2	3	5
Washington	3	2	5
Vancouver	1	3	4
Boston	1	2	3
Buffalo	2	1	3
Kansas City	1	2	3
Los Angeles	0	3	3
Toronto	0	3	3
California	2	0	2

New York Islanders	2	0	2
Chicago	0	1	1
Detroit	0	1	1
Montreal	0	1	1
Total	28	33	61

12 Ron Flockhart.

On December 6, 1981, the Flyers met the Blues in the Spectrum and game were tied, 2–2, after the first period as Bill Barber tallied twice. After the Flyers increased their lead to 4–2 after two periods on goals by Mark Botell and Glen Cochrane, they increased the lead to 6–2 when Ron Flockhart scored eight seconds apart at 5:10 and 5:18 of the third period to turn the game into a rout. Brian Propp and Bobby Clarke added goals to make it an 8–2 final. Flockhart had played 14 games with the Flyers the preceding season. He spent the next two seasons in a Philadelphia uniform before he was traded early in the 1983–84 season to Pittsburgh.

It was also a team record for the two fastest goals until it was broken five years later when Dave Brown and Brian Propp scored seven seconds apart against the Blues. It was matched twice (1988–89) and (2012–13).

The Flyers set a new club record of six seconds in the final game of the 2017–18 season. Needing a victory against the Rangers at the Wells Fargo Center to make the playoffs, they held a 2–0 lead in the second period when Michael Raffl scored at 17:53 and Claude Giroux added his second goal of the game six seconds later. Giroux added a goal in the third period for his first NHL hat trick as the Flyers skated to a 5–0 win. He set personal highs with 34 goals and 68 assists for 102 points. Giroux was the sixth Flyers players to score 100 or more points in a season.

13 Tim Kerr.

Tim Kerr scored 54 goals for the second straight season in 1984–85 and three of them came in the space of 2:27 as the Flyers beat St. Louis at the Spectrum, 7–2, in the eighth game of the year. The Flyers were leading, 4–1, when Kerr scored at 12:22, 12:45, and 14:49 of the third period. Kerr also scored a goal in the first period and he would go on to set the club record for the most times scoring four goals in a game in one year with three. His second four-goal game came against the Red Wings at the Spectrum in a 7–5 win. Kerr scored two goals each in the first and second period including three straight staking the Flyers to a 5–2 lead.

Kerr had his third four-goal game against the Capitals in a 5–4 victory at Washington. He scored the Flyers' first four goals before Brian Propp scored the game-winning goal with two seconds left in the game. Kerr went on to set the club record for the most times scoring four goals in a game with four. His final four-goal game came two seasons later in a 5–1 win over Chicago at the Spectrum and his four goals were all consecutive.

The closest anyone has come to tying Kerr's record was John LeClair, who had three four-goal games as a Flyer. LeClair had his four-goal games in three different seasons, and two came against his former team, the Canadiens. His first was at the CoreStates Center in 1996–97 as the Flyers beat Montreal, 9–5. Two seasons later, LeClair turned on the red light four times again as the Flyers beat Vancouver, 6–2, at the Wachovia Center. LeClair's last four-goal game came in the third game of 2002–03 at the Forum in Montreal as the Flyers won, 6–2.

14 Rick MacLeish.

The Flyers pounded the Islanders at the Spectrum, 8–2, on February 13, 1973, as Rick MacLeish scored four goals at 6:30, 6:57, and 13:25 in the second period and at 6:17 of the third period. Less than a month later, MacLeish became the first Flyer to score four goals in a game twice in the same season in a 10–0 rout against Toronto at the Spectrum.

15 Tim Kerr.

One thing a fan should always try to do when attending a game is to be on time and in your seat for the opening faceoff. You just never knew when the red light might come on. On March 7, 1989, Tim Kerr didn't waste any time staking the Flyers to a 1–0 lead against Edmonton at the Spectrum when he scored a goal eight seconds into the game. The Flyers jumped out to 4–2 lead after one period but the Oilers tied the game with two goals in the second period and the game ended in a 4–4 tie.

The fastest the Flyers ever scored two goals to start a game was against the Islanders at Long Island on October 26, 2002. Justin Wilson scored 16 seconds into the contest and Michal Handzus 15 seconds later. At the time, this was the third quickest a team scored two goals to start a game in NHL history. The Flyers added three more goals in the first period and skated away with a 6–2 win.

16 Reggie Leach and Bill Barber, 1976.

The Flyers were shooting for their third consecutive Stanley Cup when the 1975–76 season got underway. The LCB line of Reggie Leach, Bobby Clarke, and Bill Barber set the league record for the most points scored in a season by one line with 322 points. The trio scored 141 goals and added 181 assists. Leach led the league with 61 goals, Barber's 50 were tied for fifth and Clarke added 30. Clarke was second in points with 119 and Barber was fourth with 112. The Flyers led the league in goals scored with 348 and were third in fewest goals allowed with 209. Wayne Stephenson was in goal for most of the season while Bernie Parent recovered from a neck injury. Clarke led the league in plus/minus rating with 83, Barber was second with 74, and Leach was tied for third with 73. Despite having a great season including the big win over the Russians, their season ended with four straight defeats. With Parent sitting on the bench and Rick MacLeish out following a season-ending knee injury, the Flyers were swept by Montreal in the Stanley Cup Finals.

17 John LeClair.

Playing on the line known as the "Legion of Doom" with Eric Lindros and Mikael Renberg, John LeClair was the sixth Flyers player to score 50 or more goals in a season and became the first player in team history to go over 40 or more goals five times. After scoring 51 goals in 1995–96, LeClair scored 50 the next season and 51 in 1997–98 season. His total dropped off to 43 in 1998–99 and 40 in 1999–2000. LeClair spent close to 10 seasons in Philadelphia after he was acquired from the Canadiens. After the league shut down for the 2004–05 season and play was getting ready to resume the following year, the Flyers were forced to part ways with LeClair due to the new salary cap regulations. LeClair, who scored 333 goals with the Flyers, was inducted into the United States Hockey Hall of Fame in 2009 and the Flyers Hall of Fame in 2014.

18 Tim Kerr with 34.

Kerr scored 34 of his 58 goals on the power play in 1985–86, setting the NHL record and it was the third of four straight seasons that he would score 50 or more goals, a Flyers record. Kerr broke Phil Esposito's record of 29 in early March against Detroit. An eye injury later that month caused him to miss four games. He scored on the power play against 15 of the 20 opponents.

Pelle Eklund assisted on 17 of his power play goals while Brian Propp assisted on 11 and Ilkka Sinisalo 10. Kerr had a hat trick alone on the power play against the Kings at the Spectrum in a 7–4 Flyers win. Five other times he had two power play goals in the same game.

TIM KERR'S POWER PLAY GOALS AGAINST EACH OPPONENT IN 1985–86

New York Islanders	6
Los Angeles	5
New Jersey	5
Pittsburgh	3
Montreal	2
New York Rangers	2
Vancouver	2
Washington	2
Boston	1
Calgary	1
Detroit	1
Hartford	1
Minnesota	1
Toronto	1
Winnipeg	1

FLYERS THAT ASSISTED ON TIM KERR'S 34 POWER PLAY GOALS IN 1985–86

Pelle Eklund	17
Brian Propp	11
Ilkka Sinisalo	10
Mark Howe	8
Doug Crossman	6
Dave Poulin	5
Peter Zezel	5
Brad McCrimmon	2
Murray Craven	1
Thomas Eriksson	1
Ron Sutter	1

19 Shayne Gostisbehere.

Shayne Gostisbehere was in his second year with the Flyers in 2015–16 when he set the club record for the most overtime goals in a season with four. Gostisbehere had played two games with the Flyers the year before and had started the 2015–16 season with the Phantoms but after 14 games, got the call to come to Philadelphia. In only his fifth game back from the minors, Gostisbehere scored his first overtime goal of the season as the Flyers beat Carolina, 3–2, at home. Four days later, he repeated it again, this time, against Nashville in a 3–2 win at the Wells Fargo Center. Gostisbehere's third overtime goal came against Carolina at the Wells Fargo Center to give Philadelphia a 4–3 victory. His fourth came in Toronto as the Flyers beat the Maple Leafs, 5–4. That season, Gostisbehere set an NHL rookie record for defensemen by collecting a point in 15 straight games.

20 Al Hill with two goals and three assists.

Al Hill was called up from the minors and made his debut against the St. Louis Blues on February 14, 1977, at the Spectrum. He scored his first goal after only 36 seconds of the first period. After the Blues tied the game, Hill scored his second goal at 11:33 and assisted on Reggie Leach's goal, the Flyers' third of the period. Bob Dailey opened up the scoring in the second period to make it 4–1 and Mel Bridgman followed with a goal as Hill picked up his second assist of the game. Hill's third assist and fifth point came in the third period when Bobby Clarke scored the Flyers' sixth goal of the game as they held on to beat St. Louis, 6–4.

Hill divided his time with the Flyers and their top farm team in Springfield that season. The following year, he was called up and spent the next four years in Philadelphia. Hill went back to the American Hockey League but did return briefly to the Flyers in 1986–87 and 1987–88. Today, Hill is a special assignment scout for the team.

21 Tom Bladon with eight points (four goals, four assists).

Tom Bladon set the NHL record for the most points scored by a defensemen in a game with eight against the Cleveland Barons at the Spectrum on December 11, 1977. The Flyers won the game, 11–1. Reggie Leach opened up the scoring in the first period before Bladon got into the act. He scored the second goal of period and added assists on goals by Don Saleski and Mel Bridgman. The Flyers added four goals in the second period as Bladon turned the red light on twice. Bladon's fourth goal made it 9–0 in the third period and he assisted on the Flyers' final two goals by Rick MacLeish and Bill Barber. The Flyers got off 52 shots with 15 in the first period, 17 in the second period, and 20 in the third period. Bernie Parent lost his bid for a shutout with only 1:15 to go in the game. Earlier that season, the Flyers posted their biggest shutout win in team history, 11–0, over Pittsburgh at the Spectrum. Bladon, who joined the Flyers in 1972–73, was traded after the season to Pittsburgh. Paul Coffey of Edmonton tied Bladon's record eight seasons later.

22 Eric Lindros with six.

The Flyers were in Ottawa to take on the Senators on February 26, 1997, and Eric Lindros had six assists to set the club record for the most in a game. He added a goal, bringing his point total to seven, one short of the club record set by Tom Bladon almost 10 years earlier. The Flyers beat

Ottawa, 8–5, and the first period was a high scoring affair as the period ended 4–4. John LeClair opened up the scoring with the first of his three goals on the evening as Mikael Renberg and Lindros assisted. After Ottawa tied it, Paul Coffey, who had been picked up in a trade from Hartford a little over two months earlier and on his way to a Hall of Fame career scored as Lindros added his second assist of the game. After the Senators came back to tie the game, 2–2, LeClair got his second goal of the game as Renberg and Lindros once again assisted. Renberg made it 4–2, as Lindros and Dale Hawerchuk picked up assists. The Senators tied the game, 4–4, as the team headed to the locker room for the first intermission.

Ottawa took a 5–4 lead in the second period but goals by Lindros and Rod Brind'Amour, assisted by Lindros and Coffey, put the Flyers ahead for good. Philadelphia put the game away with two goals in the third period as Renberg got his second of the night and LeClair completed his hat trick with Lindros getting his sixth assist of the game.

23 Wayne Simmonds.

The Flyers had nine different players score two goals in the season opener, but no one had picked up a hat trick until 2017–18 when the Flyers went to San Jose and beat the Sharks, 5–3. Tied, 2–2, after the first period, Simmonds scored his first goal of the night assisted by Shayne Gostisbehere and Jacob Voracek. The Sharks tied the game, 3–3, early in the third period before Simmonds broke the tie at 9:27 with Voracek and Gostisbehere adding the assists. With 36 seconds left in the game, Simmonds got his third goal of the night on an empty net with Sean Couturier getting the assist.

Rosaire Paiement had been the first Flyers player to score two goals on opening night in the team's second season in a 3–2 loss at Boston. Bill Barber led the way with the most two-goal games on opening night in club history with three, all consecutive beginning in 1980–81 as the Flyers beat Pittsburgh at the Spectrum, 7–4, and for the only time, the Flyers had three players record two goals in the opener as Yves Preston and Al Hill each scored twice. The following season, Barber had two goals against Detroit as the team tied, 2–2, at the Spectrum. A year later when Barber had his third straight two-goal game in the season opener, the Flyers set the record for the most goals scored in the opening game, as they beat Quebec, 9–5. Barber also holds the club record for the total most goals scored in season openers with 10, followed by Bobby Clarke with six and John LeClair with five.

24 Bobby Clarke and Ross Lonsberry were the first and Dave Poulin was in three games.

The Flyers were riding high during the 1973–74 season when they met the Red Wings in early February at the Spectrum and skated away with an easy 12–2 win. Clarke and Lonsberry each scored a goal in the opening period as the Flyers took a 5–1 lead. Clarke got his second goal in the second period as the Flyers increased their lead to 7–1. Lonsberry got the next two goals to start the third period and Clarke got the club's 12th goal of the game with 4:27 to go.

Ten years later, Dave Poulin and Ilkka Sinisalo each had a hat trick in the same game as the Flyers set the club record for the most goals in a game with 13 against the Penguins. The Flyers had two players score hat tricks in the same game twice the next season. Brian Propp and Sinisalo led the Flyers in a 13–2 win at the Spectrum over Vancouver and later that season, the Flyers beat the Capitals, 9–6, at the Spectrum. Tim Kerr was joined by Poulin for the fourth time the Flyers had two players score hat tricks in the same game. Kerr and Poulin did it again two seasons later as the Flyers defeated the Islanders at home, 9–4. The sixth and most recent time came in 2007–08 when Joffrey Lupul and R. J. Umberger each had a hat trick, the first for both players. at the Wachovia Center as the Flyers beat the Penguins, 8–2.

25 Tim Kerr with 17.

Tim Kerr signed with the Flyers as an undrafted free agent in 1979–80 and spent 11 seasons with the team but injuries slowed him down over the years. He scored 363 goals in 601 games and had 17 hat tricks with the Flyers. He also set the club record for the most hat tricks in a season with five in

1984–85. Kerr also had three hat tricks in each of the next two seasons. After one season each with the Rangers and Hartford, he retired at the age of thirty-three. When the Flyers went to the Stanley Cup Finals against Edmonton in 1985 and 1987, Kerr was sidelined due to injuries. Kerr also set Flyers record for the most consecutive times scoring 50 or more goals in a season with four hitting a personal high with 58 in both 1985–86 and 1986–87. The following season, after missing the final two rounds of the Stanley Cup playoffs, he only played in eight games after undergoing five shoulder operations in 14 months. Kerr came back with 48 goals in 1988–89.

26 Bobby Clarke with 32.

Bobby Clarke set the record for the most short-handed goals for the Flyers with 32. He tied for the league lead with five with Ralph Stewart of the Islanders in 1973–74 and tied for the league lead with Lorne Henning, also of the Islanders, in 1976–77 with six. Bill Barber led the league with six in 1978–79, Reggie Leach tied with Anders Kallur of the Islanders with four the next year, and Mike Richards led the NHL with seven in 2008–09. The club record for the most short-handed goals in a season was set by Brian Propp with seven in 1984–85. Mark Howe tied Propp's record a year later and Mike Richards also matched it in 2008–09.

27 Rod Brind'Amour with 484.

Rod Brind'Amour was acquired from the St. Louis Blues along with Dan Quinn for Murray Baron and Ron Sutter in 1991. During his eight full seasons in Philadelphia, he played in all but three of their 624 games and established the club record playing in 484 straight games. An ankle injury forced

him to miss the first 34 games of the 1999–2000 season. After returning to the lineup and playing in 12 games, he was traded to Carolina with Jean-Marc-Pelletier and a 2000 second-round draft pick for Keith Primeau and a fifth-round draft pick. He is one of only seven players in team history to have 60 or more assists in a season with 62 in 1993–94 and 61 assists two seasons later. Brind'Amour later was the captain of the Carolina Hurricanes and helped lead his team to the Stanley Cup championship in 2006. Overall, Brind'Amour played 20 years in the NHL in four different decades. He was inducted into the Flyers Hall of Fame in 2015.

28 Mel Bridgman.

Pat Quinn was beginning his first full season behind the bench in 1979-80 when he named Bobby Clarke an assistant coach. NHL rules stated that an assistant coach who was also a player could not be the captain. For the first time since the middle of the 1972–73 season, Bobby Clarke would not have the letter "C" on his sweater. Mel Bridgman wore the "C" for two years. Bill Barber took over as captain in 1981–82 and began the following year as captain, but when Clarke went back to being just a player, he resumed his role as captain until he retired. Clarke at twenty-three years old had been the youngest captain in NHL history when he was appointed during the 1972–73 season. Eric Lindros later became the youngest Flyers captain at twenty-one. All told, the Flyers have had 18 captains.

29 Blazers, Firebirds, and Phantoms

The Phillies and Eagles at one time or another had another team playing their sport in Philadelphia at the same time. There were two and sometimes three baseball teams in Philadelphia in the nineteenth century. The Phillies and later the A's, who set up shop in 1901 and were the most popular team in the City of Brotherly Love until 1949 when the Phillies, also known as the Whiz Kids, took over. The A's moved to Kansas City after the 1954 season. There was another football team in town in 1965 and 1966, the Bulldogs of the Continental Football League, but they were a minor-league team that was not in direct competition with the Eagles.

The World Football League started up in 1974 and the Bell played in Philadelphia the first year and part of 1975 before the league folded. Spring football started up in 1983 with the formation of the United States Football League but their games were played in the spring and summer. The Stars played in Philadelphia for two years and won one championship before they moved to Baltimore.

Beginning in 1960, the American Football League was founded and a year later, the American Basketball League was formed. The American Basketball League set up shop in Philadelphia for one year during the 1962-63 season after the Warriors moved to San Francisco and before the 76ers moved to Philadelphia from Syracuse. Philadelphia teams never had any completion in the city after the A's left until the World Hockey Association started play in the fall of 1972 when the Blazers were formed. They played in the Civic Center which was not built for hockey. The first NHL player that signed a WHA contract was Bernie Parent who was with Toronto at the time. He originally signed with the Miami Screaming Eagles, but that club never got off the ground. The Blazers stayed one year before going to Vancouver. Next was the Firebirds in the North American Hockey League who won the championship in 1976. The league folded after the following season. The Firebirds moved to the American Hockey League for two years before moving to Syracuse.

The CoreStates Center opened in 1996–97 season, but the Spectrum was still available for hockey and the Flyers moved their American Hockey League team there. The Phantoms won the Calder Cup championship in 1998 and 2005. When the Spectrum was torn down, the team moved to Adirondack until the PPL Center was ready in Allentown and the Phantoms moved there in 2014–15.

30 1-d, 2-g, 3-f, 4-b, 5-a, 6-e, 7-h, 8-c

Eric Desjardins started his NHL career with the Montreal Canadiens in 1988–89. On February 9, 1995, the Flyers acquired him from the Canadiens along with Gilbert Dionne and John LeClair for Mark Recchi and a third–round draft choice. He stayed in Philadelphia through the 2005–06 season and by the time he hung up his skates, he was the Flyers' second-leading scorer among defensemen with 396 points, second to Mark Howe. He was elected a Second Team All-Star at the end of the 1998–99 and 1999–2000 seasons and was selected to play in the All-Star Game in 1996 and 2000. Desjardins won the Barry Ashbee Trophy given annually to the Flyers' most outstanding defensemen a record seven times including a record six straight years. Desjardins was inducted into the Flyers Hall of Fame in 2015.

Ron Flockhart nicknamed "Flocky Hockey," came up for 14 games during 1980–81. In the following two seasons, the center picked up 72 and 60 points. Eight games into the 1983-84 season, Flockhart was traded to Pittsburgh along with Andy Brickley, Mark Taylor, and first- and third-round draft picks for Rich Sutter and second- and third-round draft picks. Flockhart played nine years in the NHL with five different teams.

Claude Giroux was the 22nd overall pick in the first round of the 2006 draft. Nicknamed "G", he played two games with the Flyers in 2007–08 and was recalled for good the following year when he played 42 games. He became the seventh player in Flyers history to record 60 or more assists in a season with 65 in 2011–12, the second-highest total that year in the NHL. Giroux was named the captain of the Flyers on January 13, 2013. He led club in scoring in 2010–11, 2011–12, 2012–13, 2013–14, 2015–16 and 2017–18. Giroux has led the Flyers in assists in seven of the past eight years and points in six.

His most famous goal came against the New York Rangers in the final game of the 2009–10 season in a do-or-die situation. The Rangers and the Flyers were tied for the eighth playoff spot in the Eastern Conference. New York got on the board when Jody Shelley scored at 3:27 of the first period. The Flyers tied the game, 1–1, in the third period on a goal by Matt Carle with Jeff Carter and Danny Briere picking up the assists. Neither team scored for the rest of the game including a five-minute overtime. The shootout began, and Briere scored first but in the second round, P. A. Parenteau scored for the Rangers. Giroux was next, and he put the puck past Henrik Lundqvist. Next up, Olli Jokinen was stopped by Brian Boucher and the Flyers were in the playoffs.

Shayne Gostisbehere was selected in the third round of the 2012 draft and is nicknamed "Ghost." He made his debut playing two games with the Flyers in 2014–15 and came up for good early in 2015–16, appearing in 64 games. During the season, he set the NHL rookie record for a defenseman by scoring a point in 15 consecutive games and became the first rookie in NHL history to score four overtime goals in a season. Gostisbehere was voted to the All-Rookie team and was the youngest winner of the Barry Ashbee Trophy as the Flyers' most outstanding defenseman.

Bob Kelly was a solid player for the Flyers for 10 years and helped the team win two Stanley Cups. Nicknamed "Hound," he was one of the team's top enforcers. Kelly was drafted in the third round by general manager Keith Allen in 1971 after he had taken Bill Clement a round earlier. Kelly broke in with the Flyers the same year. He was traded to the Capitals after the 1979–80 season. In his second season in Washington, he played in only 16 games and retired. Today, Kelly is an Ambassador of the hockey for the Flyers.

Reggie Leach, who was known as the "Riverton Rifle," was acquired from the California Seals five days after the Flyers won the 1974 Stanley Cup. In eight years in Philadelphia, he scored 306 goals, seventh in club history, and is second among right wingers behind Tim Kerr, who scored 363. Leach led the club in goals four times. Twice, he scored 50 or more goals in a season with 61 in 1975–76 and 50 in 1979–80. He was selected for the NHL All-Star Game in 1976 and 1980, and was voted a Second Team All-Star in 1975–76. He also won the Conn Smythe Trophy as the Most Valuable Player in the Stanley Cup Playoffs in 1976. After 1981–82, he signed with the Detroit Red Wings as a free agent and played one season with them. Leach was inducted into the Flyers Hall of Fame in 1992.

After the Flyers had been getting intimidated by the St. Louis Blues, Ed Snider ordered the front office to do something about it and the sooner, the better. Left wing Dave Schultz, known as "The Hammer," put a quick stop to the team being pushed around. Don Saleski, Bob Kelly, and Moose Dupont joined him, and the Broad Street Bullies were formed. Nobody dared to start anything with this team. Schultz was drafted in the fifth round in the same draft as Bobby Clarke in 1969. He played his first game with the Flyers in 1971–72 and went on to lead the league in penalty minutes four times, setting the NHL record for the most in a season with 472 in 1974–75. Schultz also showed he could do more than fight and take penalties. He scored the game-winning goal in the fourth game of the 1974 playoffs against the Flames in overtime as the Flyers swept the Flames. He was the fourth Flyers player to score a goal in overtime, but the first to do it in the final game of a series. Right before the start of the 1976–77 season, he was traded to Los Angeles. Schultz was inducted into the Flyers Hall of Fame in 2009.

Wayne Simmonds was acquired from Los Angeles on June 23, 2011. Nicknamed "Simmer," he scored 20 or more goals in a season six times for the Flyers, with a high of 32 in 2015–16. The right wing led the club in goals scored for four straight seasons beginning in 2013–14. In his first season with the Flyers, he recorded his first "Gordie Howe hat trick" (a goal, an assist and a fight). Simmonds was voted to play in the 2017 All-Star Game where he won MVP honors.

OVERTIME

We head into the award winners and look at highlights including two Stanley Cups, the big win over the Soviets, Most Valuable Players, Hall of Fame players, those Flyers that reached 1,000 points and much more.

(Answers begin on page 123)

1 How many times has a Flyer won the Hart Memorial Trophy for being the Most Valuable Player in the National Hockey League?

2 How many Flyers have won the Conn Smythe Trophy for Most Valuable Player in the Stanley Cup playoffs?

3 How many Flyers coaches have won the Jack Adams Award for Coach of the Year?

4 How many Flyers players have been inducted in the Hockey Hall of Fame?

5 Who is the only Flyers goaltender to score a goal?

6 Who is the only Flyers player to score his first NHL goal on a penalty shot?

7 True or false: When the Flyers beat the Soviet Red Army team in 1976, they were the only NHL team to beat them.

8 When the Flyers set the NHL record for the longest unbeaten streak, how many games did they play without a loss?

9 How many games long is the Flyers longest winning streak?

10 How many times have the Flyers won 50 or more games in a season?

11 The Flyers record for the most players scoring 20 or more goals in a season is eight. How many times have they accomplished this?

12 What four players scored their 1,000th NHL point playing for the Flyers?

13 Bobby Clarke holds the Flyers record for the most assists and points in a career. Against which team did Clarke have both the most assists and points?

14 Bill Barber holds the club record for the most goals scored with 420. What team did he score the most goals against?

15 Who were the only two Flyers players to win the MVP of the All-Star Game?

16 Who was the first Flyers player selected to play in the All-Star Game?

17 Who was the first Flyers player to score two goals in the All-Star Game?

18 Who was the first Flyers player selected to the end of season All-Star Team?

19 Who was the first Flyers coach to win the All-Star Game?

20 Who was the first team that the Flyers swept in the Stanley Cup playoffs?

21 Who was the first Original Six team that the Flyers met in the playoffs?

22 The Flyers were the first expansion team to beat one of the Original Six teams in the Stanley Cup playoffs. Which team did they beat?

23 What is the Flyers club record for the most consecutive playoff wins at home?

24 Who holds the club playoff record for goalies for the most shutouts in one series?

25 What Flyers player tied the playoff record for the most short-handed goals in a game? He also tied the record for most short-handed goals in a period.

26 In the sixth and final game of the Wales Conference Finals against Quebec at the Spectrum in 1985, the Flyers were down two men. Who scored the first 3-on-5 goal in Flyers playoff history?

27 Which Flyer tied the NHL playoff record for the most goals in one period?

28 Who is the only Flyers player to score a goal in overtime in the seventh game of a playoff series?

29 What Flyers player tied an NHL record by scoring two short-handed goals on the same power play in a playoff game?

30 How many Flyers scored the most points in one postseason year?

31 Who holds the club record for most points scored in a playoff game?

32 How many Flyers coaches made the Stanley Cup Finals in either their first season or first full season behind the bench?

33 Only one former Philadelphia Rambler played on the 1975 Stanley Cup champions. Who was he?

34 How many players from the first Flyers team in 1967–68 were on their two Stanley Cup championship teams?

35 When the Flyers clinched the Stanley Cup in 1974 and 1975, what two players scored the Cup–winning goals?

OVERTIME ANSWERS

1 Four times.

Only four times among two players has a Flyer won the Hart Memorial Trophy for being the NHL's Most Valuable Player. Bobby Clarke won the award in 1973 in his fourth season when he scored 37 goals and added 67 assists for 104 points. Clarke had finished 10th in 1971 and eighth in 1972. After finishing fourth in 1974, Clarke came back and won it in 1975 and 1976. In 1975, Clarke scored 27 goals with 89 assists and 116 points. In 1976, when the LCB line set an NHL record for most points scored with 323, he had 30 goals, 89 assists, and 119 points and added his third Hart Memorial Trophy. He finished second in 1977 to Guy Lafleur.

Eric Lindros won the Hart Memorial Trophy in 1995 in his third year. Before the season began, he was named captain. Due to a lockout, the season was shortened to 48 games. Lindros scored 29 goals, added 41 assists and had 70 points and led the Flyers back to the playoffs for the first time since 1989. In his rookie season, in 1993, Lindros had finished ninth in the voting and was voted to the NHL All-Rookie Team.

2 Three—Bernie Parent, Reggie Leach, and Ron Hextall.

Bernie Parent won the Conn Smythe Trophy in 1974 and 1975 as the Flyers won the Stanley Cup both times, but Reggie Leach in 1976 and Ron Hextall in 1987 won their awards in a losing cause.

Parent was in goal for all 17 games of the 1974 playoffs. He had two shutouts, one against the Rangers and one against Boston in the sixth game when the Flyers clinched their first Stanley Cup. In five other games, he gave up only one goal and his goal-against average was 2.02 for the playoffs. The Flyers swept Atlanta and outshot the Flames in three of the four games. Against the Rangers, the Flyers only outshot New York twice while the shots were even in two games, of which the Flyers won both. Boston had home-ice advantage in the finals and were the favorite to win their third Stanley Cup in five years. The Flyers hadn't beaten the Bruins in the Boston Garden since 1967, but Bobby Clarke's overtime goal in Game Two there gave Philadelphia a big boost. The Flyers only outshot the Bruins in games three and four. In Game Six when the Flyers wrapped up the Stanley Cup championship, Boston got off 30 shots. Parent made a great kick save on Ken Hodge's slap shot late in the game to preserve the shutout.

The following season, Parent became the first player to win the Conn Smythe Trophy two straight years and for the second year in a row, he posted a shutout in the final game. The Flyers swept the Maple Leafs in the opening round as Parent shut out Toronto in games two and three. Next up were the Islanders and during the warmups for Game One, Parent was injured when a shot hit him just above the knee. Wayne Stephenson took over in goal for the first two games and shut out the Islanders in Game One. Parent came back and blanked the Islanders in Game Three, but New York refused to quit and won three straight to even the series. The Islanders' dream of coming back from another 3–0 deficit as they had in the previous round against Pittsburgh was extinguished as the Flyers won Game Seven, 4–1. They outshot the Islanders in six of the seven games and in the final game, took 35 shots to only 14 for New York.

The Flyers won the first two games in the finals over Buffalo at the Spectrum and lost the next two to the Sabres in Buffalo. In Game Three, fog formed in the arena due to lack of air conditioning. Game Five at the Spectrum was all Flyers as they jumped to a 5–0 lead. Parent lost his bid for a shutout when he gave up his lone goal of the game at 14:02 of the third period. Once again in the final game, Parent came up with a great save when the Sabres had a two-on-one late in the second period. The game remained scoreless until the Flyers scored two goals in the third period. The Sabres outshot the Flyers in four of the six games. Both years, Parent was voted to the NHL First All-Star Team. He shared the Vezina Trophy with Tony Esposito of Chicago in 1974 and won it outright in 1975. Parent gave up only an average of 1.89 goals per game in the playoffs.

Attempting to win their third straight Stanley Cup, the Flyers fell in four straight games to Montreal in 1976. Reggie Leach set the NHL playoff record for the most goals in one playoff year with 19. Leach had six goals in the first round as the Flyers defeated Toronto in seven games. In the next series against Boston which the Flyers won in five games, he had a goal in each of the first four games and in the fifth game, scored five times, which tied the playoff record for most in a game and it was the most ever for a Flyers in a game, regular season or playoff. In the finals, they lost the first three games by one goal and the final game by two goals. The Flyers scored only nine goals against the Canadiens, but Leach had four of them. Leach set the NHL record for the most consecutive playoff games scoring a goal with ten. He started his streak in the final four games against the Maple Leafs, extended it to nine games by scoring in five straight games against the Bruins and scored in the opening game against the Canadiens. His streak was stopped in Game Two of the finals in Montreal. Overall, he had at least one goal in 13 of 16 playoff games. Leach also led the league in goals scored with 61 during the regular season.

In 1987, the Flyers met Edmonton in the Stanley Cup Finals for the second time in three years. This time around, the Oilers had home-ice advantage. To get to the finals, Edmonton knocked out Los Angeles in five games, swept Winnipeg in four, and ousted Detroit in five games, playing a total of 14 games. Meantime, the Flyers had to play 19 games to advance to the finals, eliminating the Rangers, Islanders, and Canadiens. Edmonton had three days off and the Flyers two before the finals got underway. Edmonton took a 3–1 series lead and looked ready to clinch it on home ice, but the Flyers won Game Five and then Game Six at the Spectrum to tie the series before dropping Game Seven in Edmonton. Hextall's great goaltending throughout the series got the Flyers to Game Seven and he was awarded the Conn Smythe Trophy. He also won the Vezina Trophy, and was voted to both the NHL First All-Star Team and the All-Rookie Team.

3 Four—Fred Shero, Pat Quinn, Mike Keenan, and Bill Barber.
The Jack Adams Award for Coach of the Year was first awarded in 1974 and the Flyers are one of four franchises to have won the award four times. Detroit was the first and the St. Louis Blues were the most recent.

Fred Shero was the winner in 1974 when the Flyers finished in first place in the West Division with 112 points, second best in the NHL. Six years later, in his first full season behind the bench, Pat Quinn won the award as the Flyers took the top spot in the Patrick Division of the Clarence Campbell Conference with 116 points, best in the NHL and 21 points more than the preceding year. When the award was given out in 1985, Mike Keenan, in his first season as Flyers coach picked up the trophy as Philadelphia led the league with 113 points. By this time, the Flyers had moved to the Prince of Wales Conference and finished first in the Patrick Division. All three coaches led the Flyers into the Stanley Cup Finals with Shero the only coach to win it all. Bill Barber won the award in 2000–01 after taking over from Craig Ramsay after the team managed only 28 points in the season's first 28 games. Over the final 54 games, the Flyers had 72 points and finished with 100 points, coming in second in the Atlantic Division. The season ended on a down note when the Flyers were eliminated in the first round of the playoffs by Buffalo in six games.

4 Thirteen players and six builders.

Six players who spent most of their career in Philadelphia are in the Hockey Hall of Fame. Bernie Parent was the first to be inducted in 1984 after playing 10 seasons in Philadelphia. Parent was clearly the greatest goaltender in Flyers history as he led the team to Stanley Cup titles in 1974 and 1975 and in those two years was as great a goaltender that there ever was. Next up was the Flyers' greatest player, Bobby Clarke, who was inducted in 1987. Three years later, Bill Barber, the Flyers leading goal scorer with 420 got the call to the Hall of Fame. It wasn't until 2011 that the next former Flyers player made the Hall of Fame when Mark Howe was selected joining his dad, Gordie in Toronto. Eric Lindros was the next former Flyer to be inducted into the Hall of Fame in 2016. He spent eight of his 13 years in Philadelphia before injuries cut short his career.

A year later, Mark Recchi, who played 10 seasons with the Flyers and set the club record for the most points scored in a season with 123, was inducted.

Seven players that spent time with the Flyers are also enshrined in the Hall of Fame. Allan Stanley (1968–69) was the first. He played 21 years in the NHL but only one season in Philadelphia. The other six were Darryl Sittler (1982 to 1984), Dale Hawerchuk (1996 to 1997), Paul Coffey (1996 to 1998), Adam Oates (2002), Peter Forsberg (2005 to 2007), and Chris Pronger (2009 to 2012).

Six men associated with the Flyers made it to the Hall of Fame as builders. The first was the team's founder and owner Ed Snider in 1988. The Flyers' first general manager, Bud Poile was inducted in 1990 followed by Keith Allen, the first Flyers coach and second general manager, who entered the Hall in 1992. Three other Flyers coaches were inducted in the Hall of Fame: Roger Neilson (2002), Fred Shero (2013), and Pat Quinn (2016).

5 Ron Hextall.

Ron Hextall had shown everyone how well he handled the stick and it was only a matter of time before he hit it into the opponent's goal. On December 8, 1987, at the Spectrum, the Flyers were leading Boston, 4–2, and the Bruins had pulled their goalie trying to close the gap but at 18:48, Hextall stopped a Boston shot and lifted it high enough and hard enough as he shot the puck the length of the ice. Hextall is also one of only two goalies (Martin Brodeur is the other) to score a goal in a playoff game. On April 11, 1989, he scored into an open net against Washington to seal an 8–5 victory over the Capitals in Game Five. The Flyers went on to win the series in six games.

6 Ilkka Sinisalo.

On October 11, 1981, Ilkka Sinisalo was playing in his second NHL game against the Penguins at the Spectrum. The Flyers were well ahead in the third period, 5–2, when Randy Carlyle was called for tripping on a breakaway at 16:39, setting up Sinisalo's penalty shot. He put the puck past Paul Harrison, extending the Flyers' lead to 6–2 for his first NHL goal. The Flyers added two more goals by Reggie Leach and Ken Linseman in the next 1:06 to win the game, 8–2.

7 True.

The hockey world stopped on January 11, 1976, when the Flyers were the final team to meet the Red Army team from the Soviet Union. During what was called Super Series '76, the team had already beaten the Rangers, 7–3, tied the Canadiens, 3–3, and defeated the Bruins, 5–2. Another Russian team, the Soviet Wings beat the Penguins, 7–4, lost to the Sabres, 12–6, beat the Black Hawks, 4–2, and the Islanders, 2–1. The prestige of the National Hockey League was at stake in the final game and it was Russia's best team against the Flyers who had won the past two Stanley Cups.

The game was scoreless when Ed Van Impe threw a body check on Valeri Kharlamov and when no penalty was called, the Red Army coach Konstantin Loktev pulled his team from the ice. When play was resumed, and a bench penalty was called at 11:21, seventeen seconds later, the Flyers took a 1–0 lead on a goal by Reggie Leach with Bill Barber picking up an assist. Four minutes and 59 seconds later, Rick MacLeish scored to put the Flyers ahead, 2–0, with Ross Lonsberry picking up an assist. Joe Watson scored a short-handed goal for the Flyers in the second period as Don Saleski and Orest Kindrachuk assisted. The Soviets got their lone goal later in the period before Larry Goodenough made it 4–1 in the third as Bobby Clarke and Gary Dornhoefer were credited with the assists. The Flyers outshot the Soviets, 49–13. Wayne Stephenson was in goal for the Flyers.

8 Thirty-five games.

The Flyers set the NHL record for the longest unbeaten streak during the 1979–80 season when they went 35 straight games without a loss. It wasn't until the 2005–06 season when the shootout was implemented that ties were no longer played. Up until this time, the longest winning streak in the NBA was 33 straight wins in 1972–73 by the Los Angeles Lakers and in baseball, the New York Giants had a 27-game unbeaten streak with 26 wins in 1916. The NHL record for the longest unbeaten streak had been set by the Montreal Canadiens who went 28 straight games without a loss in 1977–78.

After winning the season opener over the New York Islanders, 5–2, at the Spectrum, the Flyers traveled to Atlanta and were soundly beaten by the Flames, 9–2. The Flyers returned home and beat Toronto, 4–3, to start the 35-game unbeaten streak. They won 25 and had 10 ties. The Flyers won 14 and had six ties at the Spectrum and on the road, they won 11 with four ties. They played every team in the NHL during the streak except Washington. The Flyers beat 18 of the 20 teams they did play and tied Chicago and Pittsburgh. The Flyers wrapped up the Patrick Division with 14 games to go. They finished 25 points ahead of the Islanders and posted a record of 48–12–20.

During the streak, Reggie Leach had the hot hand with 25 goals and 15 assists for 40 points while Brian Propp was next with 39 points, scoring 20 goals and adding 19 assists. Bill Barber had 38 points on 20 goals and 18 assists.

PLAYER TOTALS DURING FLYERS' 35-GAME UNBEATEN STREAK

	Goals	Assists	Points
Reggie Leach	25	15	40
Rick MacLeish	21	13	34
Brian Propp	20	19	39
Bill Barber	20	18	38
Ken Linseman	9	24	33
Paul Holmgren	9	11	20
Dennis Ververgaert	8	9	17
Mel Bridgman	7	12	19
Bobby Clarke	6	30	36
Bob Kelly	6	8	14
Al Hill	6	5	11
Bob Dailey	5	11	16

Norm Barnes	4	19	23
Behn Wilson	3	11	14
Jimmy Watson	2	8	10
John Paddock	2	5	7
Mike Busniuk	1	11	12
Tom Gorence	1	6	7
Moose Dupont	0	5	5
Frank Bathe	0	1	1
Dennis Patterson	0	1	1
Total	155	242	397

Pete Peeters and Phil Myre split time in goal for 79 of the 80 games that season. During the 35-game unbeaten streak, Peeters had 14 wins and four ties and Myre had 11 wins and six ties. For the season, Peeters was 29–5–5 and recorded the team's only shutout while Myre went 18–7–15. Rick St. Croix was in goal for one win. Peeters set the club record for the longest undefeated streak by a goaltender in a season with 27 games, winning 22 and tying five others. It was the second longest undefeated streak in NHL history at the time.

9 Thirteen straight wins in 1985–86.

The Flyers had started the 1985–86 season by splitting their first four games before they faced off against the North Stars at the Spectrum and came away with a 7–3 win. Moving onto Chicago, the Flyers beat the Black Hawks, 5–2. They returned to home ice for the next two wins, 3–0 over Hartford and 7–4 against Vancouver. Next up were two games in Canada. First, they beat the Canadiens in Montreal, 5–4, and defeated the Nordiques, 5–3, in Quebec. Back at the Spectrum, the Flyers beat

Los Angeles, 7–4, and then traveled to Madison Square Garden and came away with a 5–2 win over the New York Rangers.

The Flyers came back to Philadelphia for three games and in the first one disposed of Chicago, 6–2. Pelle Lindbergh was in goal and no one knew it at the time, but it would be his last game. The Flyers followed up and beat Boston, 5–3, to run their winning streak to 10. Early the following morning, Lindbergh was in a serious car crash which took his life. The Flyers' next game was against Edmonton, the team they fell to in the Stanley Cup Finals the previous year. Bob Froese was scheduled to start in goal but suffered an injury, so Darren Jensen was called up from the Hershey Bears. He had only played one game the previous year with Philadelphia. The Flyers went on to beat the Oilers, 5–3, on a very emotional night. They next visited Hartford and beat the Whalers, 5–2, making it 12 straight. The club record 13th straight win came over the Islanders, 5–4, in overtime at the Spectrum on Murray Craven's goal. Two days later on Long Island, New York beat the Flyers, 8–6, snapping the streak.

10 Five times.

Winning 50 games in the NHL in a season is similar to winning 100 in baseball. The first time the Flyers won 50 or more games was in 1973–74 when they captured 50 games, winning their final game of the season, 6–2, at the Spectrum over Minnesota. The Flyers had clinched the West Division with four games to go. The NHL schedule was 78 games long, four more than when the Flyers entered the National Hockey League.

Two more games were added on the schedule the following season, and the Flyers won 51 games, winning their final two games of the season, 4–1, over the Islanders on the road and 6–2 at the Spectrum over the Flames. The NHL changed the structure of the league that year. The teams were grouped into two conferences, the Prince of Wales and the Campbell. Each conference had two divisions. The Flyers were placed in the Patrick Division of the Campbell Conference and finished first by 25 points over the Rangers and had home ice throughout the playoffs. The Flyers again won 51 games in 1975–76, taking two of the final three games, defeating Washington, 11–2, and Buffalo, 5–2, at the Spectrum. They lost their final game of the year to the Rangers in New York and had the second most points in the league with 118, a club record.

The Flyers went over 50 wins in both 1984–85 and 1985–86 and had home-ice advantage throughout the 1985 playoffs and were the second-highest seed for the 1986 playoffs. Both years, the Flyers ended the regular season with a five-game winning streak. Washington finished behind the Flyers both times, by 12 points in 1984–85 and by three points the following year.

11 Three times—1975–76, 1976–77, and 1982–83.

In the early years of the franchise, the Flyers were never noted for being a high-scoring team. It wasn't until the 1975–76 season, when they were going for their third straight Stanley Cup that Philadelphia had eight players score 20 or more goals in a season. Reggie Leach set the club record and led the league in goals scored with 61 followed by Bill Barber with 50 and Bobby Clarke had 30. Gary Dornhoefer was next with 28 followed by Orest Kindrachuk with 26. Rookie Mel Bridgman had 23 while Rick MacLeish, who had his season cut short due to a knee injury, had 22 in 51 games. Don Saleski added 21.

The following year the Flyers again had eight players with 20 or more goals. MacLeish led the way with 49 followed by Leach with 32. Clarke was next with 27 and Dornhoefer had 25. Ross Lonsberry joined the 20-plus goal team that year with 23 followed by Bob Kelly and Saleski, each with 22, and Barber had 20.

It wasn't until 1982–83 that the Flyers again had eight players with 20 or more goals. Darryl Sittler, who was in his first full season with the club after being acquired from Toronto, led the club with 43 goals followed by Brian Propp with 40. Ron Flockhart was next with 29 and Barber put 27 into the net. Clarke followed with 23 while Ray Allison and Ilkka Sinisalo each had 21 and Mark Howe, in his first season with the Flyers, had 20.

12 Bobby Clarke, Darryl Sittler, Mark Recchi, and Jeremy Roenick.

Bobby Clarke was the first of the four players to reach 1,000 points in a career but the only one of the four that played his whole career in Philadelphia. On March 19, 1981, the Flyers were leading Boston at the Spectrum, 4–0, when Clarke got his 1,000th point when he scored a goal 31 seconds into the third period with an assist from Reggie Leach, who had been a teammate when they played juniors for the Flin Flon Bombers. He was the 15th NHL player to reach 1,000 points and just missed by fifteen days of being the 14th when Guy Lafleur of Montreal beat him to the 1,000-point plateau. The Flyers went on and won the game, 5–3. Clarke finished his career with 358 goals, 852 assists, and 1,210 points. He played three more seasons before he retired and became the club's fourth general manager.

Darryl Sittler was the second player to reach 1,000 points while playing with the Flyers and the 17th in NHL history. He had been acquired from Toronto in a trade on January 20, 1982. Exactly a year later on that date, the Flyers were meeting Calgary in the Spectrum and Sittler had 998 career points. The Flyers were down, 1–0, in the first period when Glen Cochrane scored to tie the game and Sittler picked up an assist. The Flyers went ahead for good on goals by Clarke and Bill Barber in the second period before Sittler scored a goal for his 1,000th point with Barber and Brad Marsh picking up the assists.

It was another eight years before another Flyers player hit the 1,000-point mark when Mark Recchi opened up the scoring at the First Union Center on March 13, 2001 at 6:54 of the first period to become the 60th player in NHL history to hit 1,000 points. Later in the game, Recchi picked up assists on goals by Michel Picard and Keith Primeau as the Flyers beat St. Louis, 5–2.

Ten months later, on January 30, 2002, Jeremy Roenick became the 63rd in NHL history to score 1,000 points and the fourth in a Flyers uniform. He got his 1,000th point at Ottawa when he opened up the scoring with Simon Gagne picking up an assist in a 3–1 loss to the Senators.

13 Bobby Clarke had the most assists against Pittsburgh with 63 and the most points against Pittsburgh with 107.

BOBBY CLARKE'S GOALS/ASSISTS/POINTS AGAINST EACH OPPONENT

	Goals	Assists	Points
	H-A-T	H-A-T	H-A-T
Atlanta/Calgary	10–7–17	18–18–36	28–25–53

Boston	14–7–21	22–22–44	36–29–65
Buffalo	5–8–13	24–19–43	29–27–56
Chicago	6–8–14	15–21–36	21–29–50
Detroit	16–10–26	33–20–53	49–30–79
Edmonton	0–3–3	7–5–12	7–8–15
Hartford	0–0–0	12–7–19	12–7–19
Kansas City/			
Colorado/New Jersey	12–6–18	25–23–48	37–29–66
Los Angeles	7–16–23	26–22–48	33–38–71
Minnesota	8–11–19	36–22–58	44–33–77
Montreal	9–8–17	18–16–34	27–24–51
New York Islanders	11–9–20	24–10–34	35–19–54
New York Rangers	16–8–24	29–19–48	45–27–72
Oakland/Cleveland	15–7–22	19–20–39	34–27–61
Pittsburgh	27–17–44	39–24–63	66–41–107
Quebec	1–3–4	8–4–12	9–7–16
St. Louis	10–4–14	32–28–60	42–32–74
Toronto	10–6–16	27–22–49	37–28–65
Vancouver	11–13–24	32–26–58	43–39–82
Washington	5–10–15	27–17–44	32–27–59
Winnipeg	3–1–4	6–8–14	9–9–18
Total	196–162–358	479–373–852	675–535–1210

PLAYERS THAT SCORED GOALS ASSISTED BY BOBBY CLARKE

Reggie Leach	159
Bill Barber	157
Rick MacLeish	44
Bill Flett	43

Bob Kelly	40
Paul Holmgren	28
Simon Nolet	26
Gary Dornhoefer	23
Tom Bladon	22
Brian Propp	19
Ross Lonsberry	18
Mel Bridgman	16
Jimmy Watson	16
Lindsay Carson	15
Behn Wilson	15
Mark Howe	14
Bob Dailey	12
Darryl Sittler	12
Moose Dupont	11
Tim Kerr	10
Ray Allison	9
Lew Morrison	8
Dave Schultz	8
Ilkka Sinisalo	8
Jean-Guy Gendron	7
Larry Goodenough	6
Orest Kindrachuk	6
Joe Watson	6
Al Hill	5
Andre Lacroix	5
Cliff Schmautz	5
Barry Ashbee	4
Rick Foley	4

Wayne Hillman	4
Greg Adams	3
Harvey Bennett	3
Serge Bernier	3
Thomas Eriksson	3
Reggie Fleming	3
Ron Flockhart	3
Brent Hughes	3
Bill Lesuk	3
Don Saleski	3
Ed Van Impe	3
Terry Ball	2
Glen Cochrane	2
Doug Crossman	2
Larry Hillman	2
Mark Taylor	2
Dennis Ververgaert	2
Norm Barnes	1
Mark Botell	1
Bill Clement	1
Bill Collins	1
Miroslav Dvorak	1
John Evans	1
Ross Fitzpatrick	1
Tom Gorence	1
Len Hachborn	1
Larry Hale	1
Earl Heiskala	1
Bob Hoffmeyer	1

Dave Hoyda	1
Rick Lapointe	1
Ken Linseman	1
Brad Marsh	1
Brad McCrimmon	1
Jack McIlhargey	1
John Paddock	1
Michel Parizeau	1
Garry Peters	1
Jean Potvin	1
Dave Poulin	1
Bill Sutherland	1
Ron Sutter	1
Total	159

14 Bill Barber scored his most goals against Pittsburgh with 37.

BILL BARBER'S GOALS AGAINST EACH OPPONENT

	Home	Away	Total
Atlanta/Calgary	11	5	16
Boston	9	9	18
Buffalo	13	5	18
Chicago	6	11	17
Detroit	15	9	24
Edmonton	6	4	10
Hartford	7	4	11
Kansas City/Colorado/ New Jersey	15	8	23

Los Angeles	15	9	24
Minnesota	13	12	25
Montreal	7	9	16
New York Islanders	13	11	24
New York Rangers	8	16	24
Oakland/Cleveland	4	6	10
Pittsburgh	20	17	37
Quebec	5	3	8
St. Louis	17	14	31
Toronto	16	8	24
Vancouver	12	13	25
Washington	13	11	24
Winnipeg	6	5	11
Total	231	189	420

15 Reggie Leach and Wayne Simmonds.

Reggie Leach, representing the Campbell Conference, took home the All-Star Game Most Valuable Award in 1980 even though his team fell to the Wales Conference, 6–3. Leach scored a goal late in the first period after the Wales had taken a 2–0 lead. The Campbell Conference tied it, 2–2, in the second period when Kent Nilsson of the Atlanta Flames scored with Rick MacLeish and Bernie Federko of St. Louis adding assists. The Campbell Conference took a 3–2 lead in the third period when Brian Propp scored a goal assisted by Leach and Phil Esposito of the New York Rangers, but the Wales scored four straight goals to win the game, 6–3.

Wayne Simmonds won the All-Star MVP in 2017, the second year that the format was changed from two teams playing a 60-minute game. Instead, it became a four-division,

three-on-three tournament that was held through a single elimination. Each game consisted of two 10-minute periods. Simmonds was selected to play for the Metropolitan Division and he scored the first two goals for his club, both unassisted, leading his team to a 10–6 win over the Atlantic Division after the Pacific Division beat the Central Division, 10–3. The Metropolitan Division beat the Pacific Division, 4–3, in the final game. The Pacific had taken a 3–2 lead but Cam Atkinson of Columbus tied it with a goal and five seconds later, Simmonds scored the game-winning goal. Even though he scored a hat trick, statistics from those games have not been applied to the NHL All-Star Game records.

16 Leon Rochefort.

Major League Baseball played their first All-Star game in 1933 and the NFL started the Pro Bowl in 1939. The NHL followed in 1947 but with only six teams, they had the Stanley Cup Champion from the previous year play the All-Stars from the other five teams before the regular season began. In 1968, the game was moved to the middle of the year. In the first year of expansion, the All-Stars played the 1967 Stanley Cup champion Toronto Maple Leafs and Leon Rochefort, a right wing, was the only Flyers player selected to the team. The format was changed to East against West the following season and Bernie Parent was the first goalie and Ed Van Impe the first defenseman from the Flyers to represent the team. In 1970, rookie Bobby Clarke was the first Flyers center to go to the All-Star Game. Bill Barber was the Flyers' first left wing to play in the game in 1975. In 1972, Simon Nolet became the first Flyer to score a goal in All-Star Game and Clarke picked up the first assist by a Flyer in 1973.

17 Brian Propp.

Brian Propp became the first Flyers player to score two goals in the All-Star Game in 1986. After the Campbell Conference opened up the scoring with a goal in the second period, Propp scored his first goal of the game for the Wales Conference with 2:04 left in the period. The Wales Conference took a 2–1 lead in the third period, but Wayne Gretzky of Edmonton tied the game, 2–2, at 17:09. Propp came back 29 seconds later to make it 3–2, but the Campbell Conference tied it with 43 seconds to go on a goal by Dale Hawerchuk. The Wales Conference won it in overtime on a goal by Bryan Trottier of the New York Islanders at 3:05. Mike Keenan was the winning coach and became the only Flyers coach to win two All-Star Games when he won his second in 1988. John LeClair (1997), Simon Gagne (2001), and Danny Briere (2011) became the next three Flyers players to score two goals in the All-Star Game.

18 Bernie Parent.

Bernie Parent was the first Flyers player named to the season-ending First All-Star Team in 1973–74 and he followed suit the following year. He was joined by Bobby Clarke in 1974–75, the first Flyers center to be selected. Clarke had been the first Flyer to make the Second Team in 1972–73. Bill Barber was their first left wing selected in 1975–76. It wasn't until 1982–83 that a Philadelphia defensemen was selected and it was Mark Howe who won the honors. The first right wing to make the team was Jakub Voracek when he was selected to the 2014–15 team.

19 Pat Quinn.

Pat Quinn was behind the bench for the Campbell Conference for the 1981 All-Star Game and five of his players were on the team: Bill Barber, Bob Dailey, Paul Holmgren, Pete Peeters, and Behn Wilson. The Campbell Conference defeated the Wales Conference, 4–1. Kent Nilsson of the Calgary Flames got the Campbell Conference off to a 1–0 lead in the first period and Barber scored to make it 2–0 on a short-handed goal with Eddie Johnstone of the Rangers picking up the assist. After the Campbell increased their lead to 3–0 in the second period, the Prince of Wales scored their only goal in the third period. Wilson closed out the scoring midway through the third period with Mike Bossy of the Islanders and Wayne Gretzky picking up assists.

Fred Shero was the first Flyers to coach in the All-Star and he also was behind the bench the most times but lost all four games. Mike Keenan was two-for-two.

20 Atlanta Flames in 1974.

The Flyers made the playoffs in four of its first six years but won only won one series. With Bernie Parent joining a much-improved team in 1974, the Flyers quickly disposed of Atlanta in four games in the first round.

Game One saw the Flyers come away with a 4–1 win at the Spectrum. Gary Dornhoefer got the ball rolling with a goal with four seconds left in the first period.

Tom Bladon made it 2–0 in the second and Orest Kindrachuk scored twice in the third with Atlanta getting their lone goal between Kindrachuk's pair. Back at the Spectrum two days later, Terry Crisp opened up the scoring for the Flyers with a first-period goal before Rick MacLeish scored a hat trick in the second period. Jimmy Watson made it a 5–1 final after the Flames got their only goal of the evening.

The teams didn't get much of a break after this game. They headed to Atlanta with Game Three scheduled the following evening and the Flyers came away with a 4–1 win. Don Saleski and Bobby Clarke scored goals in the first period. After the Flames got on the board after the first intermission, MacLeish made it, 3–1, Flyers and Bill Barber's goal in the third period made it a 4–1 final. Two days later, the Flyers closed out the sweep, but had to go to overtime to do so and they also had to go without their coach. Fred Shero went for a walk after the third game and was allegedly mugged. He was sent home to recuperate and Mike Nykoluk, the first assistant coach in NHL history, took over behind the bench. Down 3–0 in the second period, Moose Dupont got the Flyers on the board. Goals by Dornhoefer and Bladon tied it in the third period and Dave Schultz won it at 5:40 of overtime.

21 Chicago Black Hawks in 1971.

The Flyers made it back to the playoffs in their fourth season after just missing out in the last game of the 1969–70 season. The first two seasons, they had lost in the first round to St. Louis. When the NHL moved Chicago from the East Division to the West Division, the Black hawks finished in first place while St. Louis finished second and the Flyers came in third, drawing Chicago in the first round. Led by Bobby Hull, who scored six goals in the first three games, the Black Hawks swept the Flyers in four games. Chicago outscored the Flyers, 20–8.

22 New York Rangers in 1974.

After sweeping Atlanta in four straight games, the Flyers moved onto to the semi-finals against the Rangers who hadn't won the Stanley Cup since 1940. New York had been back to the Stanley Cup Finals twice since then, losing in seven games to Detroit in 1950 and six games to Boston in 1972. The Flyers opened the series at the Spectrum by shutting out New York, 4–0, as Bernie Parent recorded his first playoff shutout and Rick MacLeish scored two goals. The Flyers won Game Two, 5–2, three nights later. The Rangers won Game Three, 5–3, at Madison Square Garden, and took the fourth game in overtime, 2–1, and it was a costly loss for the Flyers as Barry Ashbee got hit in the eye with a puck, ending his playing career. Back at the Spectrum for Game Five, it was all Flyers as they beat the Rangers, 4–1 as MacLeish scored twice, but the Rangers forced a Game Seven back in Philadelphia when they won the sixth game, 4–1.

The Rangers opened up the scoring in the first period of the seventh game, but MacLeish tied the game 57 seconds later. The Flyers went ahead for good in the second period on goals by Orest Kindrachuk and Gary Dornhoefer. After the Rangers closed to 3–2 at 8:49 of the third period, Dornhoefer scored his second goal of the game just 12 seconds later. The Rangers got their final goal of the period with 5:26 left, but Parent closed the door as the Flyers moved onto to the Stanley Cup Finals.

23 Thirteen straight home playoff wins.

In their first four playoff appearances in 1968, 1969, 1971, and 1973, the Flyers record at the Spectrum was 4–9 which also included six straight losses, three straight to St. Louis in 1968 and 1969 followed by two losses to Chicago in 1971 and the first game against Minnesota in 1973. The Flyers lost their last two home playoff to Montreal in the next round.

When the Flyers went back to the playoffs in 1974, they swept Atlanta in four games, starting with two at home. Next up, the Flyers won all four home playoff games against the Rangers. Boston met the Flyers three times in the finals at the Spectrum and the Flyers won all three. Returning to the playoffs in 1975, the Flyers won two home games against Toronto in a four-game sweep and in the next round beat the Islanders in the first two games. When the team returned to the Spectrum for Game Five, the Islanders stunned the Flyers, 5–1, ending their 13-game home winning streak in the playoffs.

24 Michael Leighton with three in 2010.

In the opening round, the Flyers eliminated New Jersey in five games with Brian Boucher in goal. The Flyers then came back from a 0–3 deficit to beat the Bruins in seven games. Boucher suffered an injury in the fifth game and Leighton saw his first playoff action as they combined on a 4–0 shutout in Boston. Moving on to the Eastern Conference semifinals against Montreal, the Flyers shut out the Canadiens in the first two games at the Wachovia Center, 6–0 and 3–0, as Leighton became the second Flyers goaltender to record back-to-back postseason shutouts. Bernie Parent was the first against Toronto in 1975. Moving on to Montreal, the Canadiens came back to win the third game, 5–2, but two days later, Leighton recorded his third shutout of the series, 3–0. The Flyers closed out the series two days later back home with a 4–2 win.

25 Bill Barber.

Bill Barber set the NHL record in 1980 for the most short-handed goals in a playoff series with three and he also tied the playoff record for the most short-handed goals in one playoff year. Barber had nine goals in the series as the Flyers beat Minnesota in five games. After losing Game One, Barber scored his first short-handed goal of the series in the second game as Philadelphia won it, 7–0, as seven different players scored. In the third game at Minnesota, Barber scored two goals in first period and added one goal in second as the Flyers jumped to a 4–0 lead. Minnesota closed to 4–3 in the third period, but Barber got his second short-handed goal of the series at 16:34 as the Flyers won, 5–3. Barber scored two goals at even strength in the fourth game. The game was tied, 1–1, in the second period when Barber put the Flyers ahead for good and he added a goal in the third period. Minnesota got back to within one goal, but the Flyers hung on for a 3–2 win. Back at the Spectrum for Game Five, Barber scored his third short-handed goal of the series putting the Flyers ahead for good, 2–1, and they went on to defeat the North Stars, 7–3.

26 Dave Poulin.

After the Flyers and Quebec split the first four games of the Wales Conference finals in 1985, the Flyers won the fifth game at Quebec, 2–1. Returning to the Spectrum for the sixth game, Rick Tocchet put the Flyers up, 1–0. The Nordiques were trying to get something rolling in the second period when they had a two-man advantage, but Dave Poulin had other plans and scored at 2:11 to make it 2–0 and the Flyers never looked back. Before the period ended, Doug Crossman picked up the Flyers' third goal and Pelle Lindbergh recorded his third shutout in the playoffs as Philadelphia moved on to the finals where they lost to Edmonton in five games. It was the second straight series that Lindbergh recorded a shutout in the final game.

27 Tim Kerr with four.

In 1985, the Flyers were meeting the Rangers for the third time in the last four years in the Patrick Division semi-finals. New York had swept Philadelphia in three games in 1983, but this time around it was the Flyers who swept the series. They won the first two games at the Spectrum, 5–4, in overtime on Mark Howe's goal and 3–1 the next night. In Game Three at New York, the Flyers were trailing, 3–2, when Kerr scored four straight goals in the second period, setting the playoff record for most in a period, and three came on the power play which also set the playoff record for the most power play goals in a period and he tied the playoff record for the most power play goals in a game with three as the Flyers held on to win the game, 6–5.

28 Joffrey Lupul.

The Flyers and Washington were meeting in the 2008 Eastern Conference quarterfinals when Jeffrey Lupul scored the Flyers' only overtime goal in the seventh game of a playoff series. The Capitals had home-ice advantage and won the first game, but the Flyers came back and won the next three games. Washington took games five and six to set up a seventh game in Washington. The Capitals took a 1–0 lead in the first period before the Flyers tied it on a goal by Scottie Upshall. Sami Kapanen put the Flyers into the lead in the second period, but Washington matched that. After a scoreless third period, the Flyers won it at 6:06 of overtime on Lupul's power-play goal as he put the puck past Crisobal Huet with Kimmo Timonen and Danny Briere picking up the assists, Martin Biron was in goal for the Flyers and he stopped 39 shots.

29 Rod Brind'Amour.

Rod Brind'Amour tied the NHL playoff record for the most short-handed goals on the same power play with two and he also tied the NHL playoff record for the most short-handed goals in a game with two against the Penguins in Game Five of the 1997 Eastern Conference quarterfinals. The Flyers were trailing, 2–1, late in the first period at home when Brind'Amour scored at 17:38 and 18:32, just 54 seconds apart. Pittsburgh tied it up, 3–3, in the second period but the Flyers added goals by John LeClair and Trent Klatt in the second period and Vinny Prospal in the third to win the game, 6–3, and the series in five games.

30 Four—Rick MacLeish, Reggie Leach, Eric Lindros, and Danny Briere.

MacLeish was the first Flyer to be the leading scorer in the playoffs and he did it back-to-back in 1974 and 1975. In 1974, he had 22 points with 13 goals and nine assists. The following season, MacLeish had 20 points (11 goals and nine assists) to lead all scorers. MacLeish was the only Flyers player to have two hat tricks in the same playoff year and his second hat trick against the Islanders in Game Seven of the semi-finals made him the only Flyers player to have a hat trick in a seventh game.

MacLeish was injured in 1976 playoffs, so he was unable to attempt to be the first to lead Stanley Cup scorers three years in a row. Reggie Leach took over top scoring honors with 24 points including a record 19 goals with five assists. He scored goals in 13 of 16 games including 10 in a row, a playoff record.

Eric Lindros led all playoff scorers in 1997 with 26 points in 19 games. He scored 12 goals to go along with 14 assists. His final goal in the playoffs came in the last game in Detroit. Trying to avoid being swept, Lindros scored the Flyers' only goal with 15 seconds left, but it wasn't enough as the Red Wings held on for a 2–1 victory.

Danny Briere was tops in the 2010 playoffs scoring 30 points. He scored 12 goals and had 18 assists as the Flyers reached the finals. Briere played a big part as they beat New Jersey in five games and defeated the Bruins in seven games, coming back from a 0–3 deficit. Next up, the Flyers defeated Montreal in five games, but lost the final series to Chicago in six games.

31 Claude Giroux with six.

The Flyers opened the 2012 playoffs by facing the Penguins in the Eastern Conference quarterfinals in Pittsburgh. After winning Game One, 4–3, in overtime on a goal by Jakub Voracek, the Flyers captured Game Two as Giroux set the club record for the most points in a playoff game with six, two short of the NHL record, scoring three goals and picking up three assists.

The Flyers trailed, 3–1, after the first period. Maxime Talbot scored the Flyers' goal as Giroux picked up his first

assist. Giroux quickly tied the game in the second period with two goals and each team added a goal before the second period ended. The Penguins took the lead, 5–4, in the third period before the Flyers scored four straight goals. Sean Couturier scored an unassisted goal to tie the game and Giroux and Pavel Kubina assisted on a goal by Jaromir Jagr which put the Flyers in the lead for good, 6–5. Couturier then picked up his second goal of the game as Giroux and Voracek picked up assists. Giroux closed out the scoring, completing his hat trick when he put the puck into an empty net with seven seconds remaining. The Flyers won the series in six games, but fell to the Devils in the next round in five.

32 Three—Pat Quinn, Mike Keenan, and Peter Laviolette.

Pat Quinn had taken over the Flyers in 1978–79, replacing Bob McCammon, who became the first Flyers coach to be fired during the season. Under McCammon, the Flyers were 22–17–11, and went 0–3–5 in his last eight games behind the bench. Under Quinn, the Flyers rebounded and went 18–8–4. The following season, when the Flyers had a 35-game unbeaten streak in Quinn's first full season, they had the most points (116) in the league during the regular season. In the playoffs, the Flyers swept Edmonton in three games and beat the New York Rangers and Minnesota in five games, setting up the final against the New York Islanders. For the second time in four years, the Flyers ran into a team that started a dynasty, as the Islanders won the series in six games and their first of four consecutive Stanley Cups.

Five years later, Mike Keenan took over the Flyers. After gaining home-ice advantage throughout the playoffs, the Flyers swept the Rangers in three games, knocked off the Islanders in five and Quebec in six. This put the Flyers into the finals against Edmonton and once again, the Flyers were meeting a team that was either starting a dynasty or had already started one. The Oilers won the series in five games for their second Stanley Cup in a row and they would make it four Stanley Cups in five years in 1987 and 1988 and five in seven years by winning in 1990.

Peter Laviolette was the third Flyers coach to get to the finals in his first year after replacing John Stevens in 2009–10 when they were 13–11–1. Under Laviolette, the Flyers went 28–24–5 and qualified for the playoffs on the last day of the season when they beat the Rangers in a shootout. They promptly disposed of New Jersey in five games. It looked as though the Flyers' season was over when they fell behind Boston in the next series, 0–3, but the Flyers rallied and won four straight to become the third NHL team to come back from that deficit. Philadelphia defeated Montreal in five games to reach the finals where they lost to Chicago in six games. Once again, they met a team starting a run of winning championships. The Blackhawks had last won the Stanley Cup in 1961, their third overall. After beating the Flyers, the Blackhawks would win the Stanley Cup again in 2013 and 2015.

33 Ted Harris.

Defenseman Ted Harris joined the Ramblers in 1956–57 and stayed in Philadelphia for two years before moving on to the American Hockey League. In his first year with the Ramblers, they finished second in the Eastern Hockey League behind the Charlotte Clippers. In the first round of the playoffs, the Ramblers defeated the Johnstown Jets in six games but lost the finals to Charlotte in seven. Montreal bought him up for four games in 1963–64 and he went on to help the Canadiens win the Stanley Cup in 1965, 1966, 1968, and 1969. He then spent time with Minnesota, Detroit, and St. Louis.

On September 16, 1974, Keith Allen purchased Harris from the Blues and in his final season in the NHL, he helped the Flyers win their second Stanley Cup.

34 Four—Bernie Parent, Joe Watson, Gary Dornhoefer, and Ed Van Impe.

Only four players from the first Flyers team were on the Stanley Cup–winning team in 1974. Bernie Parent, Joe Watson, and Gary Dornhoefer had been taken from the Bruins in the expansion draft in 1967 and Ed Van Impe had been selected from Chicago. Parent was traded to Toronto in 1970–71 and returned in 1973–74. Barry Ashbee, Terry Crisp, and Ross Lonsberry had played with the Bruins before coming to Philadelphia and Rick MacLeish had been drafted by Boston but never played a game with the Bruins.

35 Rick MacLeish and Bob Kelly.

The Flyers took the ice in Game Six of the 1974 Stanley Cup Finals leading the Bruins, three games to two. One more win and the championship would be the team's first in only their seventh year after entering the National Hockey League in 1967–68. The Flyers had made it to the Stanley Cup Finals by knocking out Atlanta in four games and the New York Rangers in seven. The Bruins, who were attempting to win their third Stanley Cup in five years, eliminated Toronto in four games and Chicago in six games. The Flyers didn't have home-ice advantage in this series and the franchise had won a total of one game at the Boston Garden in seven years. When the Flyers won Game Two on Bobby Clarke's goal at 12:01 in overtime, after losing Game One in Boston, the momentum switched to Philadelphia's side.

They then won games three and four at the Spectrum before falling in Game Five.

Philadelphia hadn't been this excited about a home game in any sport since December 26, 1960, when the Eagles beat Green Bay at Franklin Field, 17–13, to win their third NFL championship. Kate Smith sang "God Bless America" for the second time that year at the Spectrum. As soon as the organ was brought out onto the ice, the fans were up and cheering. Boston had two power play opportunities in the first period but failed to capitalize. The Flyers had their first power play chance when Terry O'Reilly went to the penalty box for roughing at 13:58. Bobby Clarke and Bobby Orr joined him in the box 24 seconds later and Rick MacLeish scored the only goal of the game with Moose DuPont assisting at 14:48. With Bernie Parent in goal, you had the feeling that one goal might be enough and as it turned out, it was. The Bruins outshot the Flyers, 30–26.

Parent did what he had been doing all season as he made a great kick save on Ken Hodge's slap shot with less than three minutes remaining in the third period. The Flyers got the puck back and Clarke had a breakaway chance. Orr grabbed him by the arm and was whistled for a penalty at 17:38. When the final horn sounded, bedlam broke loose not only in the Spectrum but throughout the Delaware Valley as the Flyers brought a championship back to Philadelphia for the first time since the 76ers won the 1967 NBA title. Over two million fans showed up for the parade the following day.

Proving that 1974 was no fluke, the Flyers made it two straight Stanley Cups in 1975 by defeating the Sabres, clinching the series in the sixth game at Buffalo, 2–0. To get to the finals, the Flyers defeated Toronto in four games and the

Islanders in seven. Buffalo sent Chicago packing in five games and eliminated Montreal in six. For the second year in a row, Bernie Parent posted a shutout in the deciding game of the finals, this time, 2–0. The game was scoreless thorough two periods, but with 11 seconds gone in the third period, Bob Kelly scored to give Philadelphia the lead. Reggie Leach and Jimmy Watson assisted on the goal. Both the Sabres and Flyers had six power play opportunities, but Parent was at the top of his game. With 2:47 to go in the game, Bill Clement, playing what turned out to be his last game with the Flyers, picked up a much-needed insurance goal with Orest Kindrachuk picking up the assist.

The Flyers became the third franchise in Philadelphia sports history to win two consecutive championships. The A's had won the World Series in 1910 and 1911 and again in 1929 and 1930. The Eagles won NFL titles in 1948 and 1949.

FLYERS SCORING AGAINST BOSTON—1974

	Goals	Assists	Points
Bobby Clarke	3	3	6
Rick MacLeish	2	3	5
Moose Dupont	2	1	3
Dave Schultz	1	2	3
Bill Flett	0	3	3
Don Saleski	0	3	3
Orest Kindrachuk	2	0	2
Bill Barber	1	1	2
Tom Bladon	1	1	2
Terry Crisp	1	1	2
Ross Lonsberry	1	1	2

Ed Van Impe	0	2	2
Joe Watson	0	2	2
Bill Clement	1	0	1
Simon Nolet	0	1	1
Jimmy Watson	0	1	1
Total	15	25	40

FLYERS SCORING AGAINST BUFFALO—1975

	Goals	Assists	Points
Bill Barber	2	4	6
Bobby Clarke	2	3	5
Reggie Leach	3	1	4
Bob Kelly	2	2	4
Rick MacLeish	1	3	4
Terry Crisp	0	4	4
Ross Lonsberry	2	1	3
Gary Dornhoefer	2	0	2
Dave Schultz	2	0	2
Don Saleski	1	1	2
Larry Goodenough	0	2	2
Ted Harris	0	2	2
Orest Kindrachuk	0	2	2
Ed Van Impe	0	2	2
Jimmy Watson	0	2	2
Bill Clement	1	0	1
Moose Dupont	1	0	1
Tom Bladon	0	1	1
Total	19	30	49

About the Authors

Skip Clayton hosts *Racing Wrap*, a weekly one-hour radio show on WBCB Levittown, Pennsylvania, and has covered sports for the ABC Radio Network for more than forty years. Clayton is also the author of *So You Think You're a Philadelphia Eagles Fan?*, and *Philadelphia's Big Five* and coauthor of *Tales from the Miami Dolphins Sideline* and *50 Phabulous Phillies*. He resides in Sellersville, Pennsylvania.

Bill Clement played 11 seasons as a center in the National Hockey League and was a member of the Flyers' Stanley Cup-winning teams in 1974 and 1975. He is currently a color analyst for NBC Sports Philadelphia.